LEARNING *to use*

POWERPOINT

Creating effective presentations

ANGELA BESSANT

Heinemann

Heinemann Educational Publishers
Halley Court, Jordan Hill, Oxford OX2 8EJ
a division of Reed Educational and Professional Publishing Ltd.
Heinemann is a registered trademark of Reed Educational and Professional Publishing Ltd.

OXFORD MELBOURNE AUCKLAND
KAMPALA JOHANNESBURG BLANTYRE GABORONE
IBADAN PORTSMOUTH (NH) USA CHICAGO

First published 2001

2005 2004 2003 2002 2001
10 9 8 7 6 5 4 3 2 1

A catalogue record for this book is available from the British Library on request.

ISBN 0 435 45411 0

Designed and typeset by Artistix, Thame, Oxon
Printed and bound in Italy by Printer Trento S.r.l

Acknowledgements
This book is so multi-faceted that it really has been a team effort and I would like to
thank all members of the team for making it possible. These include the staff at
Heinemann Educational and in particular Pen Gresford and Gillian Burrell for all their
hard work and commitment; Tasha Goddard of TAG Publishing Services; my daughter
Gemma for the illustrations.

I would like to thank the contributors to the PowerPoint presentation *Milton Keynes* on
the CD-ROM.

> Music: Bespokeallstars@hotmail.com
> Selected Photographs: Milton Keynes Council
> Video Photography: Michael Francis
> Voiceover: Gemma Bessant.

Thanks are due to all past and present learners and colleagues who have been so
enthusiastic about the book and have been ever keen to try it out. However, special
thanks must go to my husband Mike who has helped through every stage; proof-reading,
trialling and encouraging. Without his help the project would have been far more
arduous and much less fun.

Screen shots reprinted with permission from Microsoft Corporation

Contents

Introduction

Computer-generated presentations are becoming more and more popular. They are used by people in all walks of life, from schoolchildren to business executives. They are included in the syllabus of many college and university courses. Microsoft® PowerPoint is a presentation graphics program that enables you to create, organise and design effective, professional-looking presentations. These can be used as handouts, overhead transparencies, 35 mm slides, presentations on a computer or projected using a multimedia projector connected to a computer. PowerPoint presentations can be broadcast and published on the Internet as well as used for online meetings. So, for instance, if you need to create a presentation that you will be presenting in person, a rolling presentation for a shop window display or a presentation that you can e-mail to interested people, PowerPoint will help you do the job with ease. All of these capabilities make PowerPoint an extremely useful office tool.

There are numerous books about PowerPoint that address the 'how to do' instructional approach. There are books about designing and delivering presentations that cover more traditional methods, such as using flipcharts and overhead projectors (OHPs) and also sometimes including presentations that are computer-generated. This book combines both of these approaches and concentrates on computer-generated presentations.

For a presentation to be successful, it must communicate information that will keep the audience interested and alert. Presentations employ different techniques depending on circumstances – for example, formal or informal, small or large audience and so on. Designing an effective presentation requires a great deal of forward thinking and planning.

Questions need to be asked, starting with …

- What do I want to say and to whom?
- What is the best way to communicate this?
- What will the presentation look like?
- How will it progress in order to emphasise the main points?
- What materials will I need?

... then more questions need to be asked about how best to achieve this aim ...

- How much information should be on one slide?
- What size font and typeface should I use?
- What colours will work best?
- Should I add graphics?
- How do I add my own drawings, photos?
- What if I want to add a company logo?
- What about presenting numerical information and charts?
- What if I want to pause the presentation?
- What about adding sound effects?

... the list goes on.

This book aims to address the topics of 'how to do' and of design, in order to best communicate with the audience.

About this book

The types of questions above are addressed from a design and hands-on perspective. There are step-by-step instructions for those who prefer to learn this way, together with **Handy References** and **Hints** for those who just want to dip in. At first glance PowerPoint appears extremely easy to use. It is. However, having a solid understanding of PowerPoint's capabilities will not only make your presentations look better, but also save you time when creating and amending them.

A PowerPoint presentation delivered using a computer is the main focus of this book. It is sometimes called a 'slide show'. This is because it consists of individual 'slides' that are displayed one after another. These do not usually end up as actual 35 mm slides. Slide is just the name given to the equivalent of a printed page.

This book gives examples using PowerPoint 2000 that is part of the Microsoft® Office 2000 software suite. There are many ways to perform a task in PowerPoint – for example, using the keyboard, mouse or menus. For simplicity, the practical exercises demonstrated usually show one method. There are, however, other methods set out in the **Quick Reference** guide at the end of the book. You will then be able to decide which is the best method for you. Other useful information can be found in the **Appendix** and there is a **Glossary** of terms. The **Appendix** also contains instructions for rapidly creating a PowerPoint presentation so that you can discover the types of things you can easily achieve. This can serve as revision or to grasp an overview of the basics before settling down to look at the chapters where topics are addressed in detail. Throughout the book there are **Handy Reference** boxes to remind you of certain topics and **Hint** boxes that offer extra tips.

In the main, this book uses default settings – that is, the settings that are automatically chosen the first time PowerPoint is used. It is easy to change settings to suit your own way of working. Instructions on how to change common settings are given in the Appendix. In PowerPoint 2000 toolbars and menus constantly update when you use them to reflect your most recent actions. To access full menus, after a drop-down menu is displayed, wait a few seconds and the full menu will appear. To access further toolbar buttons, click on the ➤ arrow button at the extreme right of the toolbar.

Getting help

This book assumes some basic PC familiarity – that is, working with Windows, menus, toolbars and so on – but requires no previous PowerPoint experience. There is a **PowerPoint Quick Reference** guide at the end of the book and useful information in the **Appendix**. PowerPoint has a **Help** menu, or pressing the **F1** key will activate **Help**. There is also an **Office Assistant**. Throughout the book, I have hidden this facility so as not to detract from the main objectives. (More details about the **Office Assistant** can be found in the **Appendix**.)

About the CD-ROM

The accompanying CD-ROM contains examples of presentations that demonstrate good and bad practices together with sufficient photographs and ClipArt for you to use when practising. It also includes presentation examples that are used in the step-by-step instructions and in the **Practise Your Skills** sections at the end of practical chapters. Details of the CD-ROM content are given in the **Appendix** as well as information on how to copy the files to your computer.

Accessing the CD-ROM

To access the CD-ROM contents:

1   Insert the CD-ROM into your CD-ROM drive.
2   From the Windows desktop **Start** menu, select: **Run**.
3   Key in the name of your CD-ROM drive – e.g. **D:**
4   Click on: **OK**.
5   The CD-ROM contents will be displayed.
6   Double-click on the folder or file that you want to access.

Chapter 1 Planning a presentation

Introduction

So, you've been asked to give a presentation and you've decided to use PowerPoint. Some typical initial reactions to this might be:

Gemma (Student)	How can I import pictures?
Mike (Manager)	I'll need to ask my PA to collect relevant information in a suitable format.
Dr B (Lecturer)	How can I get out of this? What's available to use already? Who is the audience? What is the aim?
Maria (Research Scientist)	How much time will I have for the presentation itself?
Anthea (Teacher)	How do I turn the presentation into a rolling, unattended one for parents' evenings?
Sam (Administrator)	How much time can I spare to produce it?
Sanjit (Marketing Director)	Can I create this presentation so that I can modify it to reuse for other customers? Can I e-mail it to our distributors overseas?

This chapter takes a general approach and provides ideas to help you through the initial planning stage. It discusses ways to communicate with the audience and addresses aspects of design.

The CD-ROM contains useful reference examples that you may not know how to access. Therefore, at this stage, some of the main points are also demonstrated in diagrams. As you become more familiar with PowerPoint you will learn how to access the sample files on the CD-ROM.

1 Getting started

Learning objectives

- Aims and objectives
- Collect information

- Equipment and venue

1.1 Aims and objectives

At this early stage it is well worth investing time thinking and making notes about the following: **What do you want to say and to whom will you be saying it?**

What do you want to say?

Think about the main message that you want to communicate – for example, you might want to present the results of some research or project; you might be selling a product and want to explain why that product is the best for the audience; in a job interview situation you might want to sell yourself by drawing attention to your expertise and experience, suggesting what a great asset you would be. Determine the main points you need to cover and try to find out the following from whoever asked you to do the presentation:

1   How long do I have to prepare?
2   What exactly is expected?
3   How long is the presentation to be?
4   How does the presentation fit in with other speakers at the same event (if there are any)?
5   Are there any similar previous events from which I can get information?
6   Is it a formal or informal event?
7   Will there be questions after the main presentation?

To whom will you be saying it?

When thinking about what you want to say, always put yourself in the audience's position and ask 'What do I want to hear?' Always try to satisfy the audience by focusing your attention on them. Find out:

1   Who will make up the audience and how many will there be?
2   What do they know about the subject matter to be presented?
3   Is the presentation subject controversial? If so, how many in the audience are likely to disagree with the presentation message? This information will help you judge whether to include additional information to back up your message.

4   Are there any confidentiality issues that need checking with management? For example, can details of the organisation's latest invention be released?

1.2 Collecting information

When you have answers to the questions above, you should be able to start forming some ideas about what to include in your presentation. Now is the time to start collecting and collating useful information, including photographs and ClipArt, from various sources. There are numerous places to find such content. These include:

- your own notes and knowledge, including using your own first-hand experience and your own drawn images and diagrams
- internal documentation and reports
- the Internet, using search engines
- CD-ROMs (including the one that accompanies this book)
- libraries, using their cataloguing systems to find relevant books, videos, research papers, journal and newspaper articles.

If you have the equipment, think about:

- scanning in photographs, drawings and charts
- taking photographs using a digital camera
- adding video clips and sound.

Always remember to make a note about the source of your information so that you can answer questions about it if it is contested. Ensure that you have complied with copyright laws. Copyright laws cover a great deal of material and you may need permission to use it for certain purposes.

PowerPoint enables you to present effectively the following different types of content:

- words
- tables
- charts
- ClipArt pictures, drawings and photographs
- media clips – movies and sound
- organisation charts.

The above list encompasses everything that you should need to communicate.

You may find that you have collected too much information. Select information that will keep your focus on key issues and that will keep your audience riveted. Keep the other information as supplementary material.

1.3 Equipment and venue

If your presentation is only to a few people, you may be able to use your computer screen to display the presentation. However, if you have a larger or more formal group it will be necessary to have a computer linked to a projection system. Book any equipment needed in good time. It is advisable to try out the presentation beforehand, using the actual equipment that you will use for the presentation so that you can check that it works without problems. This will also make you feel more confident with the technology.

Ensure the venue for your presentation is booked. It will help if you get to know the venue. Try not to have a venue that is too large for an event. Ensure that the venue is suitably laid out so that you can stand beside your presentation, thus avoiding having to turn your back on the audience. Check that everyone can see the slides and that the text is large enough to be read from all parts of the room.

Check the possibility of background noise – for example, from corridors, telephones and so on – and do your best to eliminate the possibility of these disrupting your presentation. Ask the audience if they would switch off their mobile phones (and don't forget your own!).

(**Chapter 9 Preparing to deliver your presentation** gives further information on giving your presentation.)

2 Communicating

Learning objectives

- Structure your presentation
- Methods of delivery

2.1 Structuring your presentation

By now you should have a good idea of what you want to say and have collected relevant information, so the next stage is to think about how best to communicate this information. We have all attended presentations that have been exceedingly boring. For instance, it can be difficult to maintain concentration when attending a presentation where speech is the only method of delivery, unless that speech is particularly gripping. A person's concentration span can be very short in such situations.

A well-structured PowerPoint presentation should immediately make the topic more interesting and varied for the audience. But beware, this will only happen if your presentation runs smoothly. When delivering presentations it is generally believed that over 50 per cent of the impact comes from what the audience sees. This visual communication comes partly from the presenter and partly from the visual aids used when presenting. Therefore it is important that you make your presentations as visually stimulating as possible.

PowerPoint gives the ability to present complex information, such as statistics and diagrams, in an easily digestible form. However, beware of ill-conceived visuals which rather than helping the presentation along, can actually be distracting and overwhelming. Keep visuals clear and simple in order to get the main message across.

Keep the following points in mind when structuring a presentation:

- Maintain the concentration of the audience.
- Keep the audience interested.
- Present information in an easily digestible form.

In order to reinforce your message it is a good idea to follow this sequence:

1   Inform the audience of what you are going to tell them.
2   Present the information.
3   End the presentation by summarising the main message again.

Your aim is to immerse the audience in the subject matter. First impressions are vitally important. You must appear comfortable and the presentation should flow seamlessly. Good planning and rehearsing in front of friends or colleagues will help reduce nervousness (see **Chapter 9**). It is vital that you grab the audience's attention from the start. If you are enthused and excited about your topic, the audience will pick up on this and respond accordingly, so try to give them this impression. Arouse audience interest in the subject by asking questions that they might want answering – for example, 'Could we have approached this project in a different way?' or 'Why is this product better than product X?'

The following lists provide some hints that you might find useful.

About the slides

- Produce your slides with care so that they look professional, are clearly readable and have a definite house style (see **Chapter 1**, **Section 3** for more about styles).
- Show the slides at the precise time they are relevant so they demand attention when necessary.
- Leave the slide displayed for long enough, so that the audience has time to take in the information (remember, this may be the first time your audience has seen the information).
- Remove the slide when it is no longer relevant.
- Do not show more than two slides in a row without speaking.
- Use slides for at least 25% of the time available.
- Use active verbs to begin lines in order to attract attention – for example, '**Increases** efficiency' and '**Looks** fashionable'.
- Use nouns to provide detail – e.g. '**Colour** – fresh and natural' and '**Texture** – smooth and silky'.

Providing additional information

- Only hand out any notes at the end so that your audience is not distracted by them.
- For a formal presentation, try to leave any questions to the end. This will ensure that the flow of the presentation is not disrupted.
- For an informal presentation, keep the audience involved by allowing questions as you go along but beware of being drawn into points that are not particularly relevant to what you want to say. Do not be afraid to say that the question is beyond the scope of the presentation.

- Do not have long pages of notes for yourself that are difficult to decipher. Instead, produce notes in PowerPoint or use prompt cards that have main points that you can enlarge on – e.g. expanding on the meaning of something to make it crystal clear; clarifying a point to ensure the audience really understands.

General

- Try to create a memorable atmosphere.
- Alter the tone of your voice to add interest.
- Use first-hand experience so that the audience gets to know a little about you.

3 Aspects of design

Learning objectives

- Overall look of slides
- How PowerPoint can help you with the design
- Practical example
- Put your design into practice

3.1 Overall look of slides

Some of the design ideas in this section may work well for you.

Layout

- Use landscape rather than portrait slide orientation. This will make the slide look less busy.
- Use no more than seven words per line.
- Use no more than four to five points per slide.
- Try to use no more than seven lines per slide.
- Put easier-to-absorb information on the top two-thirds of the slide and use the bottom for logos, dates and so on.
- Leave a margin of at least 1.5–2 cm all around the slides.
- Do not leave too much blank space since it can look uninspiring and unfriendly. Fill it with a relevant graphic, preferably one that will help with the text (see Figure 1.1); or a word with letters arranged to portray meaning (see Figure 1.2); or add shadow to some text (see Figure 1.3).

Slow   Fast

Figure 1.1 *Using an appropriate graphic to reinforce a message*

TWISTED

Figure 1.2 *Letters arranged to portray a meaning*

Figure 1.3 *Adding shadow to text*

- Use special effects, but make sure that they do not detract from the main message.
- Do you want to show all the information simultaneously or reveal it in stages? – e.g. various text-revealing effects can be applied; bar charts can be built up bar by bar.
- Does it all fit well on one slide or should you leave out information or create another slide?

Formatting

- Lower case is more restful.
- Avoid fancy lettering.
- Use sans serif fonts, as they are simple and unfussy. Serif fonts are good for normal printed text but not so clear for presentations (see **Chapter 3** for more information about fonts).
- Font size guide: 18 pt minimum size; 28 pt about right for most uses; 36 pt for main headings.
  (You may want to use larger sizes. You will not have complaints that the presentation is too legible, but you *will* have complaints if it is hard to read. However, anything larger than 60 pt is probably too large!)

Colour

- Use no more than four colours.
- Red will bring lettering or graphics forward to make it stand out.
- Blue will make lettering or graphics recede.
- Use colours to give a strong contrast – e.g. light colours on a dark background or dark colours on a light background.
- Very bright backgrounds – e.g. bright red – can be hard on the eyes.
- Avoid red and orange together.
- Colour-blind people have trouble with red and green.
- Choose a colour scheme or a theme to match your presentation content:
  - professional reds and greys or professional blues and greys for a serious tone for a corporate message or your computerised CV
  - cool green and blue for a cultured look
  - warm colours – orange, red and yellow for a friendly relaxing effect
  - greens and browns for an earthy, natural look
  - primary colours for a childlike fun look
  - vibrant and bright colours for a sporty look
  - imaginative colours for an arty look (if you dare!).

You will find examples of using these colours on the CD-ROM PowerPoint files **Accountants**, **Playgroup**, **Cosy Cafe**, **Art Debate**, **Swimming**, **Village Show** and **Academic Reading Rooms**.

Always ask yourself these questions:

- Is the slide appropriate?
- Is it the best way of getting the message across?
- Does it flow well?

You will find examples of good and bad designs on the CD-ROM that illustrate the recommendations above. The PowerPoint file **Good and bad practice** shows examples of layout. The PowerPoint file **Colour** deals with colour. You may find that you will not truly see the effects until you view the slide shows. **Note:** Colours and fonts may vary depending on your computer's capabilities.

If you do not currently have access to a computer or are new to PowerPoint, some slides are reproduced below so that you can judge different effects for yourself. You will also be able to view them later on a computer as you progress through the book.

Examples of good and bad practice

This presentation has good colour contrast – i.e. a dark background with light text.

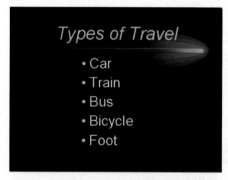 

Figure 1.4 *Lower case or upper case? These slides show the same information. Lower case is considered to be easier to read on slides and is more restful on the eye*

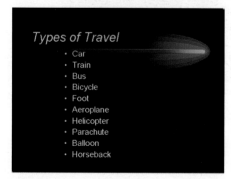

Figure 1.5 *This slide has too many bullet points. Try to use no more than four or five per slide*

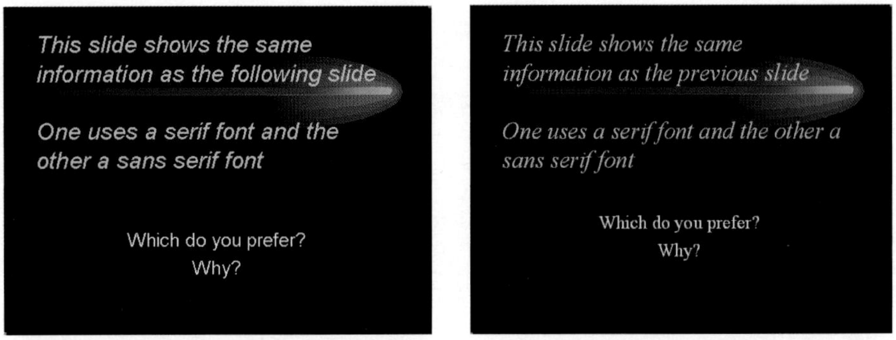

Figure 1.6 *Sans serif fonts are considered to be clearer than serif fonts on slides*

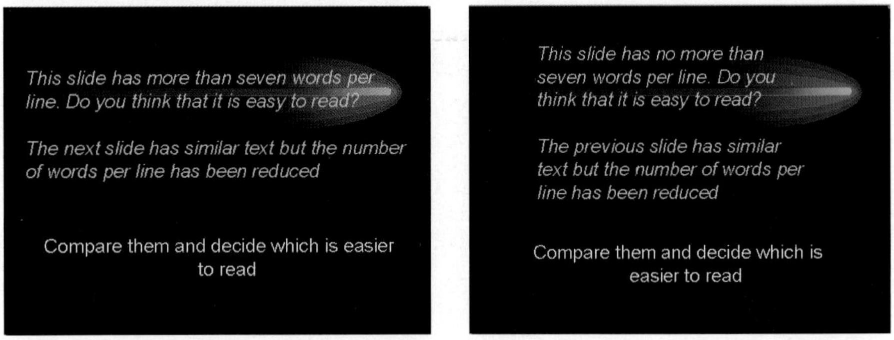

Figure 1.7 *The first slide has too many words per line. Try to use no more than seven. Leave a margin of 1.5–2 cm on all sides as in the second slide*

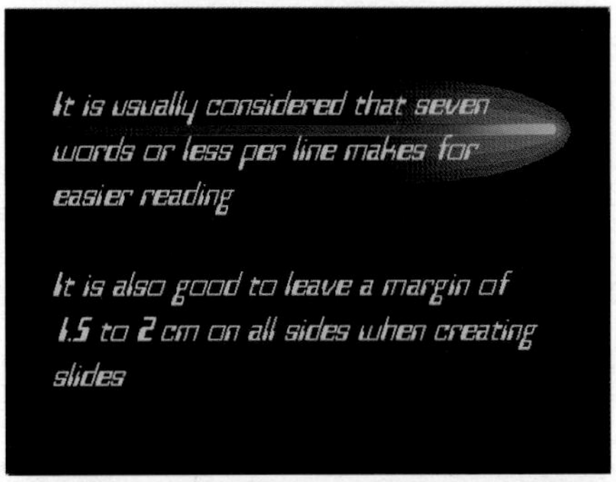

Figure 1.8 *Try to avoid fancy lettering. It is too difficult to read*

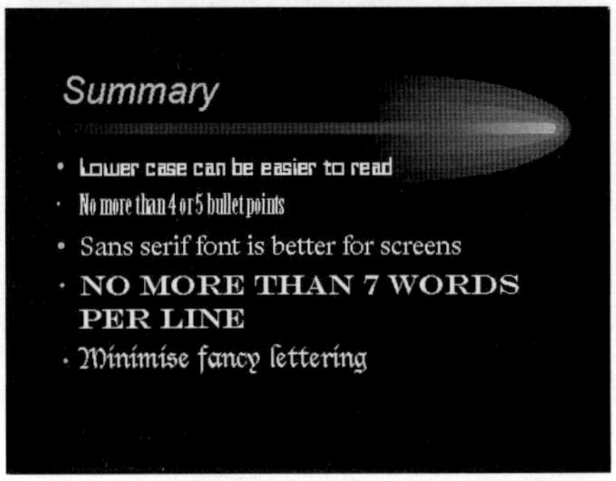

Figure 1.9 *This slide has too many different fonts*

Use of Colour

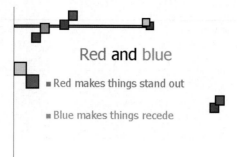

Figure 1.10 *Red and blue*

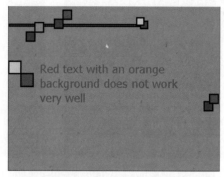

Figure 1.11 *Red on orange*

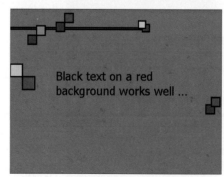

Figure 1.12 *Red and green*

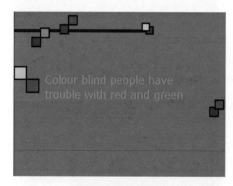

Figure 1.13 *Red and black*

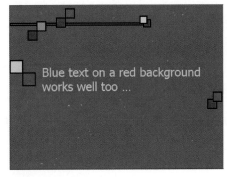
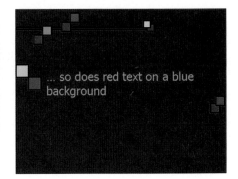

Figure 1.14 *Blue and red*

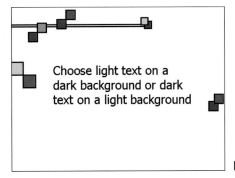

Figure 1.15 *Light and dark*

3.2 How can PowerPoint help you with the design?

You do not have to be an experienced designer to produce top-notch slides. PowerPoint has a good range of themes that you can apply, together with WordArt (fancy lettering) and clip art (prepared artwork). You can set up a **Master slide** with the main components of the design that will appear on every slide. This will give excellent overall coherence to the presentation.

PowerPoint also comes with a **Style Checker** where you can set options for it to check for visual clarity which you may or may not find useful. You will find the **Spellchecker** extremely useful too. It is so embarrassing to be giving a presentation when you notice an obvious spelling error that you had overlooked when concentrating on the content (but remember that the spellchecker has limited abilities and you should always proof-read your work carefully).

PowerPoint's special effects can be extremely effective – for example, building up bar charts bar by bar, and building up bulleted lists line by line.

Consider the following example: As part of your presentation you want to present the number of students registered on college courses. The raw data is:

Art	208
Science	150
Business	130
IT	300
Catering	60
Engineering	50

How would you present this data so that it is more interesting and easy to understand and assimilate by the audience? Would they go away from the presentation remembering what has been presented? If you present it in words alone, it might be difficult for the audience to easily understand the data. They might get the figures muddled or fail to understand the relevance of one figure to another. Look at the PowerPoint slides shown in Figure 1.16 and Figure 1.17.

Which do you think is clearer? I suspect that, from **Figure 1.17 Slide 2**, you would have instantly noticed that IT had the most students registered. Sorting the data into numerical order has further refined this point. Building up the chart column by column could make it even more effective. (See the CD-ROM, PowerPoint file **Numerical data** for chart effects.)

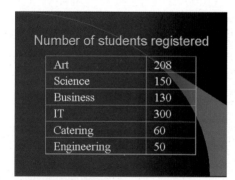

Figure 1.16 *Slide 1*

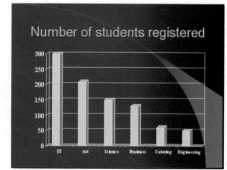

Figure 1.17 *Slide 2*

3.4 Putting your design into practice

As you progress through or dip into the following chapters you will see for yourself how your presentation can be brought to life by incorporating some of the ideas set out in this section. By now you must be looking forward to creating your own presentations so, go for it!

Chapter 2 Beginning PowerPoint

Introduction

This chapter gives a practical run through of how to create a very basic, text-only, three-slide PowerPoint presentation. It shows you two methods of achieving this. As a result you will have an overview of how PowerPoint operates. Before you begin, it is worth becoming familiar with some of PowerPoint's terminology.

A PowerPoint presentation consists of a number of *slides* (pages) that you design and create and are then able to display either on a computer or via a computer attached to a projection system as a *slide show*. While creating the slides you can also create *presenter notes*, *handouts* and an *outline* of the presentation. All of these are saved together in the same PowerPoint presentation *file*. (The file can be saved in a number of different formats depending on how you intend to use it – for example, a different version of PowerPoint or for viewing on the Internet.) There are advantages to this, in that you have all the information in one file, thus saving extra work and duplication. There are options that enable printing the slides in 35 mm format and as overhead transparencies, presenter notes, handouts or outlines. There are further printing options, which provide adjustments to suit your requirements.

The slides can be given a common look with the aid of *master slides* (these allow you to set out the design you want and then automatically apply it to all of the slides in the presentation). PowerPoint contains *wizards* and professionally designed *templates* to assist you.

You are not able to key in text directly onto a slide (as you would on a page in Word for example). Instead PowerPoint presents various *AutoLayouts* as a basis for each slide. All of these (except **Blank AutoLayout**) contain *placeholders* in which to insert the content.

The **AutoLayout** that you choose will be determined by what elements you want to appear on the slide. The elements on PowerPoint slides are called *objects*. These can include text, clip art, graphics or charts. Most **AutoLayouts** have placeholders for title text (the main heading for the slide) and body text (the main detail) that is in the form of a *bulleted* list of main points.

Note: The **Glossary** of terms at the back of the book provides more detail about terms italicised above, as well as serving as a refresher when you are working through the book.

1 PowerPoint basics

Learning objectives

- Load PowerPoint
- Modify toolbars and menus
- Access **Help**
- Create a slide
  - **AutoLayouts**
  - Types of view
  - Placeholders
- Create a new slide
  - About bullets
- Create a new blank slide
  - Add text boxes
- Add notes to slides
- Save the presentation
  - Save in other formats
- Close a file and exit PowerPoint

1.1 Loading PowerPoint

Exercise 1

Load PowerPoint.

Handy reference

Loading PowerPoint
Start menu,
Programs,
Microsoft PowerPoint

METHOD

From the **Start** menu, select: **Programs**, **Microsoft PowerPoint** (see Figure 2.1) *or* double-click on the 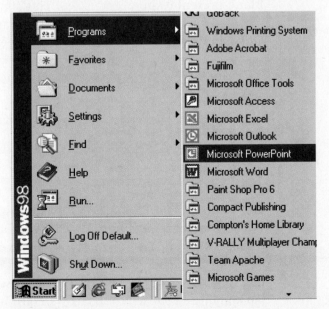 **PowerPoint** shortcut icon if you have one. Either method results in the PowerPoint window being displayed on screen (see Figure 2.2).

Figure 2.1 *Loading PowerPoint*

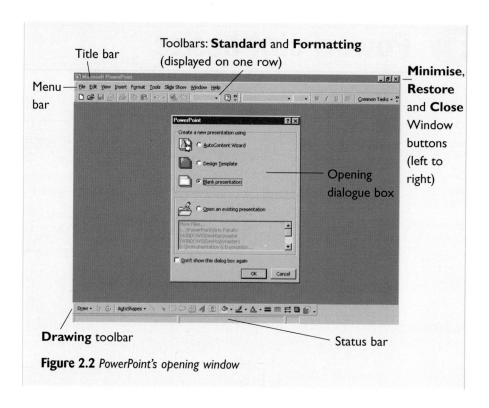

Figure 2.2 *PowerPoint's opening window*

PowerPoint's Opening dialogue box

AutoContent Wizard	This guides you through presentation creation, using a set design and set content and output (of your choice). You can then adapt this to your own needs.
Design Template	This allows you to select a design for your presentation. You then add slides and content.
Blank presentation	This allows complete freedom of design and content.
Open an existing presentation	This opens a presentation that already exists so you can run, review and amend it as you want.

1.2 Modifying toolbars and menus

Toolbars

The **Standard** and **Formatting** toolbars display (by default) on one row. To access other toolbar buttons, click on the ⏷ **More Buttons** button. It is quite useful to leave them as they are so that you have more room to work on your slides. If you do want to modify the toolbar display, from the **View** menu, select: **Toolbars**, then **Customize**. Click on the **Options** tab and make your selections. PowerPoint has other toolbars that you will meet as you progress through.

Menus

If a menu item is not immediately visible, wait a few seconds for the full menu to appear or click on the ![down arrows] down arrows to reveal the full menu.

Menus and toolbars will adjust as you work to display recently accessed options.

ScreenTip

When you hover the mouse over a toolbar button, a **ScreenTip** appears to tell you the name of that button. Locate the **Undo/Redo** buttons now. These are very useful if you want to make changes to your most recent actions.

1.3 Accessing Help

Note: Throughout this book, the **Office Assistant** facility has been hidden so as not to distract from the main objectives. (More information about the **Office Assistant** can be found in the **Appendix**.)

If you find that you require further information about a topic there are several methods. From the **Help** menu, select: **Microsoft PowerPoint Help** or click on the ![?] **Microsoft PowerPoint Help** button or press: **F1**. The **Microsoft PowerPoint Help** window is displayed (see Figure 2.3).

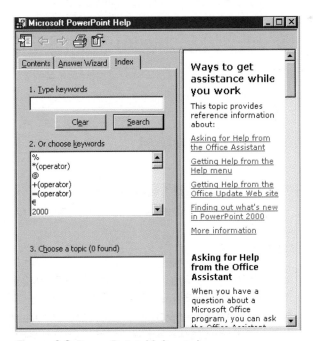

Figure 2.3 *PowerPoint Help* window

You can select any of the following tabs:

- The **Contents** tab displays a list of help topics. By clicking on a topic, a display of that topic will appear.
- The **Answer Wizard** tab allows you to key in a question and then click on: Search. The topic will then be highlighted in the contents list and the topic displayed.
- The **Index** tab allows you to key in key words and click on: **Search**. Again the topic will be highlighted and displayed.

1.4 Creating a slide

Exercise 2

Create slide 1.

METHOD

1 Click on: the **Blank Presentation** option button, then on: **OK**. The **New Slide** dialogue box appears (see Figure 2.4).

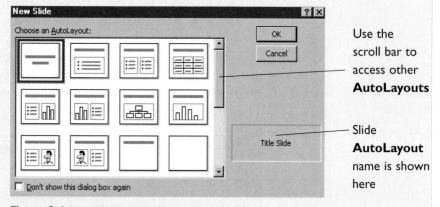

Use the scroll bar to access other **AutoLayouts**

Slide **AutoLayout** name is shown here

Figure 2.4 *New Slide dialogue box*

Information

Slides

PowerPoint uses the word *slides* for each page created, even for production of paper printouts or overhead transparencies.

2 The many different **AutoLayouts** are displayed for you to choose from. To give an idea of the sort of slides that you can create, have a look at them by clicking once on each in turn. (If you have double-clicked by mistake, click on: the 🗋 **New** button.) Notice that the **AutoLayout** name changes accordingly. Use the scroll bar to access other **AutoLayouts**. In this case click the slide **AutoLayout** at the top left – **Title Slide** (it may already be chosen). Click on: **OK**.

3   This chosen first slide is displayed in **Normal View** (see Figure 2.5).

Note: If your display looks different you may not be in **Normal View**. Click on: the **Normal View** button.

Outline pane

Drag pane borders to alter pane sizes as appropriate

Slide Views (**Normal View** far left is selected)

Slide number

Slide pane

Notes pane

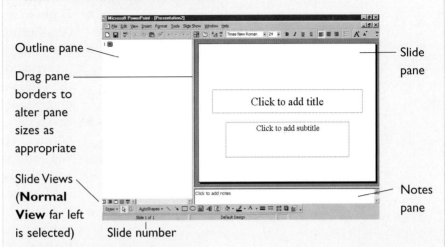

Figure 2.5 *Slide in Normal View*

Information

Slide Views

The slide is displayed in **Normal View**. View buttons are shown in Figure 2.6.

Normal View	Contains three panes: **Outline**, **Slide** and **Notes**. The pane sizes can be adjusted by dragging the pane borders. **Normal View** displays slides individually and can be used to work on or view all parts of your presentation. The **Outline** pane gives an overview of your presentation (currently there is only one slide). The **Notes** pane allows you to input any notes that you want to make about the slide. As you will discover, this will be helpful when delivering a presentation. Use this view or **Slide View** to create and edit slides.
Outline View	Displays an outline of your presentation. You can enter or review the text in your presentation in this view.
Slide View	Displays one slide at a time. Use this view or **Normal View** to create and edit slides.

Slide Sorter View	● You can view all your slides in this view as miniatures (small versions or thumbnails). ● Zoom in and out for more or less detail using the **Zoom Control**. ● Sort slides into a different presentation order by clicking on the slide you want to move and dragging it to a new location. ● Add a new slide by placing the pointer between the slides where you want the new slide to appear and clicking on the **New Slide** toolbar button. ● Delete a slide by selecting it and pressing the **Delete** key. Use the **Undo** toolbar button to reinstate the deleted slide.
Slide Show View	Shows your slides on a full screen, as they will appear when you set a slide show in motion. Select the first slide. Click on: the **Slide Show** button. To view the next slide, press: **Page Down**. When all the slides have been viewed you will be returned to the previous view. (This view will be covered in more detail in **Chapter 7**.)

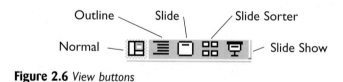

Figure 2.6 *View buttons*

The different views are shown below (see Figure 2.7).
Note: Slide Show View currently displays a blank screen because there is no content yet. Press: **Esc** to exit from **Slide Show View**.

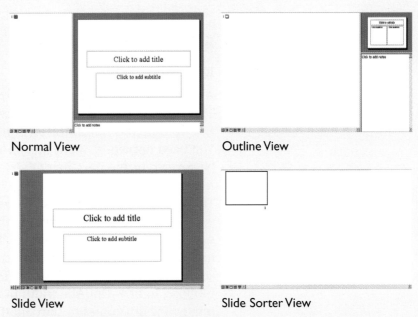

Normal View   Outline View

Slide View   Slide Sorter View

Figure 2.7 *The different views in PowerPoint*

Hint

Moving between slides

When you have created more slides, use the ◀ | ▶ arrow (bottom left) to move from slide to slide *or* use the **Page Up/Page Down** keys *or* click on the relevant slide.

4   Change to **Slide View** by clicking on the ▣ **Slide View** button. The slide is shown as in Figure 2.8. It has two pre-set placeholders (boxes with dotted-line borders in which to enter your text).

Placeholders

Figure 2.8 *Slide View*

Information

Placeholders

Placeholders are boxes that are automatically displayed on a new slide. **Blank AutoLayout** is an exception since it has no placeholders. You can enter text, graphics and other objects into placeholders.

5   In the slide pane, click in the top placeholder (**Click to add title**) and key in **Learning PowerPoint**.
6   Click in the bottom placeholder (**Click to add subtitle**) and key in your name.

Information

Keying in text

A wavy red line may appear underneath some of the text. This means that you have spelt a word incorrectly or that the word used is not in the dictionary – e.g. a surname. You need not worry about this for now. Spellchecking will be covered in the next chapter.

Title and subtitle can also be referred to as heading and sub-heading. Body text is usually the text that follows the sub-heading. PowerPoint bases its default text formats on its default *master slides*. Placeholders are preformatted with a particular size and font type, style and size. If your text is too long to fit within the width of the placeholder, the text will wrap around to start another line in the placeholder. You will need to press the **Enter** key to start a new line manually. (You will learn more about master slides in **Chapter 4**.)

1.5 Creating a new slide

Exercise 3

Create a second slide in the presentation.

Handy reference

Creating a new slide
Click on: the New Slide button.

METHOD

1   Click on: the New Slide button.
2   The **New Slide** dialogue box is displayed. This time select: **Bulleted List AutoLayout** (see Figure 2.9).

Information

Bullets

A bullet is used as a way of emphasising text. It is a symbol – e.g. ● ■ ☺ or other character or picture (that you can customise), that is placed on the same line immediately preceding the start of text.

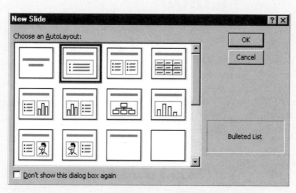

Figure 2.9 *Selecting **Bulleted List AutoLayout***

4 Click on: **OK**.

5 The second slide is displayed (see Figure 2.10).

There are now —
2 slides in this
presentation

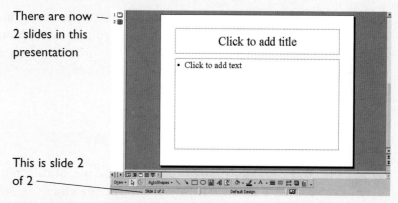

This is slide 2
of 2 —

Figure 2.10 *Second slide in presentation*

6 Click in the title placeholder and key in the text: **Advantages of using PowerPoint**.

7 Click where it reads **Click to add text**. Key in the text: **Makes topic more interesting and varied**. Press: **Enter**.

8 Another bullet appears. Key in the text: **Presents complex information clearly**. Press: **Enter**.

9 Another bullet appears. Key in the text: **Helps to provide structure**.

Note: If you have pressed **Enter** by mistake, a new bullet will have appeared. Click on: the ☰ **Bullets** button to remove the unwanted bullet.

This completes the second slide.

(1.6) Creating a new blank slide

Exercise 4

Create a third slide using **Blank AutoLayout**. Add the text: **This slide was created using the Blank AutoLayout**.

METHOD

1 Proceed as above, this time selecting: **Blank AutoLayout**.
2 On the **Drawing** toolbar, click on: the 🔲 **Text Box** button.
3 Using the mouse, position the cross hair where you want the top left of the text box to be. Hold down the left mouse button and drag out a text box. Release the mouse button.
4 Key in the text in the box. The box will automatically enlarge to ensure that all the text is displayed.

You now have three slides in the presentation.

1.7 Adding Notes to slides

You can add notes to slides to remind you of relevant information. These notes can be printed and act as prompts when you present the slides to an audience. The notes that you make do not show on the slide itself.

Exercise 5

Add the following notes to slide 2:

Maintains interest by the use of different media. Presents graphical information, bar charts, pie charts.

Handy reference

Adding Notes to slides
In **Outline View**, select relevant slide. Key in notes in bottom right-hand pane.

METHOD

1 Change to **Outline View**.
2 Select slide 2 by clicking on its icon in the left-hand pane.
3 Click in the bottom right-hand pane (**Click to add notes**) and key in the notes.

1.8 Saving the presentation

Exercise 6

Save the presentation with the file name: **Learning**.

Handy reference

Saving the presentation
File menu, **Save As**.

METHOD

1 From the **File** menu, select: **Save As**.
2 The **Save As** dialogue box appears (see Figure 2.11).

3   Click on the down arrow in the **Save in** box. From the drop-down list, select where you want to save the file and key in the file name in the **File name** box.

4   Click on: **Save**.

Figure 2.11 *Saving a presentation*

Information

Saving files in other formats

You can save your presentation file in many different formats by clicking on the down arrow in the **Save as type** box. Click on the file type you want and then on:**Save**. (See the **Appendix** for more details on different file formats.)

Examples

● Save in a different version of PowerPoint
● Save to present on the Internet
● Save in generic format (Outline/RTF)

Now that you have created a three-slide presentation, it is worth looking at the different views. In **Slide Show View**, remember to press **Page Up/Down** to move between slides.

1.9 Closing and exiting PowerPoint

Exercise 7

Close the file and exit PowerPoint.

Handy reference

Closing the file
File menu, **Close**.
Exiting PowerPoint
File menu, **Exit**.

METHOD

I   From the **File** menu, select: **Close**
2   From the **File** menu, select: **Exit**.

2 Creating a presentation in Outline View

Learning objectives

- About **Outline View**
- Create a presentation in **Outline View**
  - Use the **Outlining** toolbar shortcut buttons
  - Shortcut keys
- Rearrange slides and text
- Delete slides

2.1 Why use Outline View?

Outline View allows you to enter text into the presentation very quickly. It is useful when developing presentations since it allows you to concentrate on the text and carry through a logical thought process. You can rearrange it as necessary.

2.2 Creating a presentation in Outline View

Exercise 1

In **Outline View**, create a presentation similar to that in Section 1, as follows:

Slide 1	Learning PowerPoint [Your Name]
Slide 2	Advantages of using PowerPoint ● Makes topic more interesting and varied ● Presents complex information clearly ● Helps to provide structure
Slide 3	This presentation was created in Outline View.

METHOD

1   Load PowerPoint and open a new presentation (as in Section 1) using the **Title Slide AutoLayout**.
2   Change to **Outline View** by clicking on the **Outline View** button (bottom left).
3   Ensure that the **Outlining** toolbar is displayed down the left-hand side. If not, from the **View** menu, select **Toolbars**, **Outlining** (see Figure 2.12).
4   The cursor is flashing next to the slide 1 icon ready for you to key in text.

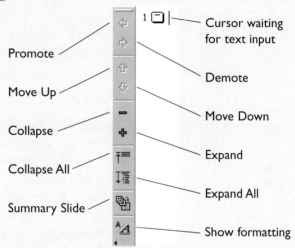

Figure 2.12 Outlining *toolbar*

Information

Outlining toolbar buttons

Toolbar button	What it does
Promote	Moves the selection up one level, to the left
Demote	Moves the selection down one level, to the right
Move Up	Moves a selection above the preceding paragraph
Move Down	Moves a selection below the next paragraph
Collapse	Displays only the title on selected slide(s)
Expand	Displays collapsed text on selected slide(s)

Collapse All	Displays only the titles of slides and hides the rest
Expand All	Displays collapsed text
Summary Slide	Creates a new slide from the titles of slides (you can select the slides you want by clicking on them while holding down **Ctrl** in **Slide Sorter View**)
Show Formatting	Shows text formatting in **Normal View**

5 Key in: **Learning PowerPoint**.
6 Press: **Ctrl + Enter** to move to the next line of the same slide. (If you pressed just **Enter**, click on: the **Undo** button.)
7 Key in: **[your name]**.
8 Press: **Ctrl + Enter** to create a new slide. (If you press **Enter** at this point you will move to the next line of text on the same slide.)
9 Key in: **Advantages of using PowerPoint**.
10 Press: **Ctrl + Enter**.
11 Key in: the bulleted list text, pressing: **Enter** after each line except the last line.
12 Press: **Ctrl + Enter** to create slide 3.
13 Key in: **This presentation was created in Outline View**.
14 Save the presentation as in Section 1 with the filename **Outline**.
15 Change to **Slide View** to see what the slides look like.

Information

Outlining toolbar and *Outline View* keys

When keying in text in **Outline View**, the text begins at the heading level. Body text is indented (demoted) under this and can go to six levels of indentation (although realistically three levels is enough on one slide). Use the toolbar buttons to promote/demote existing text.

Outline View useful keys

Ctrl + Enter	demotes text
Enter	creates a new slide
Enter	stay at the same level
Shift + Enter	removes bullets

2.3 Rearranging slides and text

Exercise 2

Move slide 2 so that it becomes the last slide in the presentation. Save the presentation with the file name: **Outlines1**.

METHOD

1   Return to **Outline View**.
2   Select the text of slide 2 and drag it to the required position.
3   Save the presentation with the file name: **Outlines1**.

2.4 Deleting slides

METHOD

Select the slide icon in the left pane and press: **Delete**.

3 Printing

3.1 Printing the presentation

Exercise 1

Print the three slides, one per page.

METHOD

1 From the **File** menu, select: **Print**. The **Print** dialogue box appears (see Figure 2.13).
2 With the **Slides** option selected in the **Print what** section, click on: **OK**.
3 Close and exit PowerPoint.

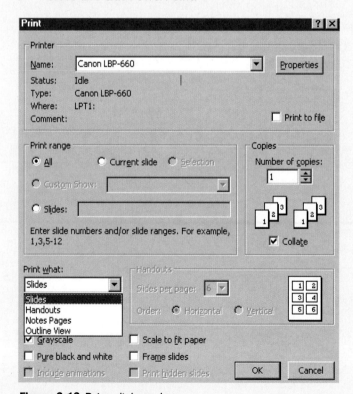

Figure 2.13 *Print* dialogue box

Information

Printing

You can print slides in various views:

- **Slides** (individual slides – one per page)
- **Handouts** (several slides on one page – you can decide the number per page in the **Handouts** section)
- **Notes Pages** (slides and notes)
- **Outline View** (the text of the slides)

You can select other options from the **Print** dialogue box:

- **Print range**: (**All**, **Current slide** or **Selection**)
- **Number of copies**
- **Grayscale** *or* **Pure black and white** (This is excellent if you are printing **Handouts**, **Notes Pages** or overhead transparencies. You can design for either landscape or portrait)

To see how your slides will print on a non-colour printer, click on: the ▨ **Grayscale Preview** (**Black and White**) button on the Standard toolbar.

Information

Using *Page Setup*

From the **File** menu, select **Page Setup**.
This enables you to set the orientation of the printout as either **Landscape** (widest edge at the top) or **Portrait** (narrowest edge at the top). You can also size the slides for different types of output.

Practise your skills

1   Create the following four-slide presentation in **Slide**, **Normal** or **Outline View**. Save it with the file name: **Elephants**.

    Slide 1   Elephants – African and Asian
                  [Your name]

    Slide 2   Common Characteristics
- Greyish to brown coloured
- Body hair sparse and coarse
- Tusks
- Trunks

    Slide 3   African Elephant
- Largest living land animal
- Larger ears than Asian elephant
- Classified as threatened

    Slide 4   Asian Elephant
- Habitat thick jungle to savannah
- Live in small family groups
- Classified as endangered

2   Add the following notes to the appropriate slides:

    Slide 2   **Common Characteristics** Two upper incisors grow into tusks. Trunk used for breathing, eating, drinking.

    Slide 3   **African Elephant** Weighs up to 7500 kg (8 tons). 3 to 4 metres (10 to 13 feet) high. Ears can be over 1 metre wide – wave their ears to keep cool.

    Slide 4   **Asian Elephant** Where food is in abundance, family groups join together to form herds.

3   Print all slides (one per page).

4   Print **Notes** pages.

5   Print **Handouts** (four per page).

Chapter 3 Working with text

Introduction

This chapter gives some ideas about how to make your text look more interesting. It also demonstrates the following:

- amending text
- working with placeholders
- further bullets and numbering
- spellchecking
- working with **WordArt**.

Learning objectives

- Open an existing presentation
- Change font
- Change font size
- Embolden, italicise and underline text
- Apply text shadow
- Emboss text

- Font effects – e.g. superscript and subscript
- Change font colour
- Copy text formatting
- Change case
- Resave an existing presentation

1.1 Opening an existing presentation

Exercise 1

Open the presentation **Learning** created in Chapter 1.

Handy reference

Opening an existing presentation
In the Opening **PowerPoint** dialogue box, select: **Open an existing presentation** *or* **File** menu, **Open**.

METHOD

1   Open PowerPoint as in Chapter 1, Section 1.
2   Click in the option button: **Open an existing presentation**.
3   Click on the file name and then on: **OK**.
4   If the file name is not visible, to locate it double-click on: **More files**.

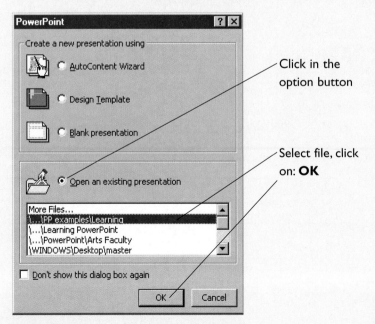

Figure 3.1 *Open an existing presentation*

Exercise 2

On slide 1, change the text to a sans serif font.

Information

Fonts

The term *font* refers to the design of the characters in a character set – e.g. Times New Roman, Century Gothic.

Serif and sans serif fonts

Serifs are small lines that stem from the upper and lower ends of characters. Serif fonts have such lines. Sans serif fonts do not have these lines. As a general rule, larger text in a sans serif font and body text in a serif font usually makes for easier reading.

Examples:

Times New Roman is a serif font.
Arial is a sans serif font.

Handy reference

Changing font and attributes
Use **Formatting** toolbar *or* **Format** menu, **Font**.

Hint

Only Arial and Times New Roman can be guaranteed to automatically display if you transfer the presentation to another computer. (See the **Appendix** for more details on transferring fonts.)

METHOD

Remember: PowerPoint bases its default text formats on its default master slide. (You will learn more about master slides in **Chapter 4.**)

1   With slide 1 displayed in **Slide View**, select the text you want to format (**Learning PowerPoint**) by holding down the left mouse button and dragging the mouse over it.

2   On the **Formatting** toolbar, the **Font** toolbar box shows the current font of the selected text (see Figure 3.2). Click on the down arrow on the **Font** toolbar box to reveal a drop-down list of other available fonts (use the scroll bar to view more). Click on any sans serif font.

3   Repeat with the text [**your name**].

Figure 3.2 *Changing font*

Exercise 3

Change the font size of the text **Learning PowerPoint** to 36 pt and the rest of the text to 28 pt.

Information

Point (pt) size

The vertical height of fonts is measured in points (pt). There are 72 points in an inch. Below are some examples of point size:

6pt

10pt

12pt

18pt

28pt

36pt

44pt

METHOD

1　Select the text to be changed.
2　Click on the down arrow of the **Font Size** box on the **Formatting** toolbar.
3　From the drop-down list, click on the point size required (see Figure 3.3).
4　Repeat for the other text on this slide.

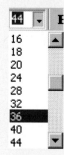

44	▾
16
18
20
24
28
32
36
40
44

Figure 3.3 *Changing font size*

Information

Font style

The font style relates to the font's characteristics. These include plain, bold, underlined, italic, shadowed and embossed. A font can have more than one of these characteristics at a time.

Exercise 4

Practise with the formatting toolbar buttons shown in Figure 3.4 to emphasise text.

METHOD

1   Select the text.
2   Click on the relevant button (see Figure 3.4).

Figure 3.4 *Emphasising text*

3   Use the **Formatting** toolbar buttons (see Figure 3.4) and/or the **Format** menu, selecting **Font** to change the font, point size, embolden, italicise or underline, apply text shadow, use subscript and superscript.

Exercise 5

Apply a text shadow to the text **Learning PowerPoint**.

Hint

You may want to zoom in so that you can see the shadow better. Use the
`57%` ▾ **Zoom** box on the toolbar. Click on the down arrow and then on the zoom required.

METHOD

1   Select the text.
2   Click on the **S** **Text Shadow** formatting toolbar button.

1.6 Embossing text

Exercise 6

Practise embossing text.

METHOD

1   Select the text to emboss.
2   From the **Format** menu, select: **Font**.
3   The **Font** dialogue box is displayed (see Figure 3.5).

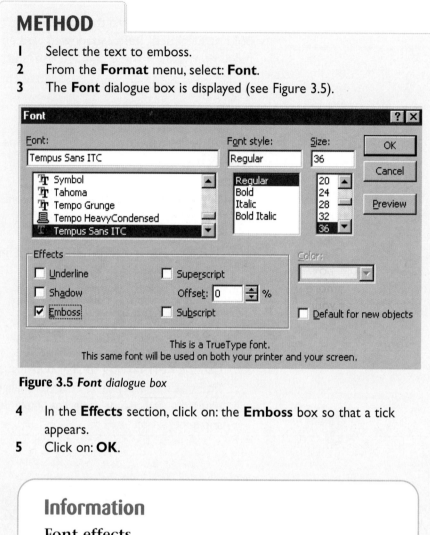

Figure 3.5 *Font dialogue box*

4   In the **Effects** section, click on: the **Emboss** box so that a tick appears.
5   Click on: **OK**.

Information

Font effects

All font effects can be achieved using the **Format** menu, **Font** box, instead of using toolbar buttons. Notice that you can also format to **Superscript** as in 100^3 and **Subscript** as in H_2O.

1.7 Changing font colour

Exercise 7

Practise changing the font colour on slide 1.

METHOD

1   Select the text to change.
2   On the **Drawing** toolbar, click on the down arrow of the A⏷ **Font Color** button. Select a colour by clicking on it or select: **More Font Colors** (see Figure 3.6).

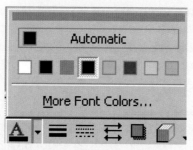

Figure 3.6 *Changing font colour*

Hint

By selecting the **Custom** tab in the **Colors** dialogue box, you can select a more exact colour for your needs – e.g. to match a company logo. **Note:** Custom colours may not reproduce exactly if you move your presentation to another computer.

3   If you select **More Font Colors**, the **Colors** dialogue box appears (see Figure 3.7).

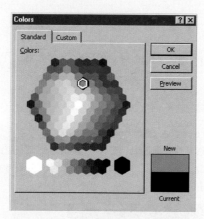

Figure 3.7 **Colors** *dialogue box*

4   Click on a colour, then on: **OK**.

1.8 Copying text formatting

Hint

To copy a format to more than one piece of text, click twice on the: **Format Painter** button. Drag the mouse over the text to copy the format to. Press: **Esc** to clear.

Exercise 8

Practise copying the format of one selected piece of text to another using the ✎ **Format Painter** button on the **Standard** toolbar.

METHOD

1   Select the text that you want to copy the format from.
2   Click once on: the **Format Painter** button.
3   Select the text to copy the format to.

1.9 Changing case

If you have made a mistake and keyed in the text in upper case or you want to use a different case, instead of rekeying all the text, you can use **Change Case** from the **Format** menu.

Exercise 9

Practise changing the text case.

METHOD

1   Select the text to change.
2   From the **Format** menu, select: **Change Case**.
3   Select from the **Change Case** dialogue box (see Figure 3.8).
4   Click on: **OK.**

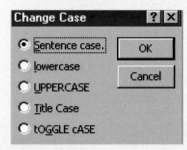

Figure 3.8 *Changing case*

1.10 Resaving a presentation with an existing file name

When you have made alterations to a presentation you can save it with its original file name by clicking on: the 🖫 **Save** button.

Note: The old version of the presentation will be overwritten so you will not be able to revert back to it.

If you do not want to overwrite it, from the **File** menu, select: **Save As** and follow the instructions in Chapter 2.

Exercise 10

Resave the presentation.

Handy reference

Resaving a presentation
Click on: the **Save** button.

METHOD

Click on: the **Save** button.

Amending and aligning text, spellchecking, working with placeholders, bullets and numbering

Learning objectives

- Insert text
- Delete text
- Search and replace
- Special characters
- Spellcheck
- Align text
- Work with placeholders

- Amend/remove bullets and numbering
- Multi-level bullets and numbering
- Line spacing
- Import text

2.1 Inserting text

Exercise 1

Using the presentation **Learning**, insert the following highlighted text to slide 1.

Learning **how to use** PowerPoint

METHOD

I   With slide I displayed in **Slide View**, position the cursor after the **g** of **Learning** by clicking the left mouse button in the appropriate place. A flashing cursor appears (see Figure 3.9).

Learning| PowerPoint

Figure 3.9 *Positioning the cursor* ⎯Flashing cursor

2   Key in a space and then the text.

Note: The text to the right of the cursor moves to make room for the new text.

Exercise 2

On the second slide of the presentation, delete the word **using** in the following sentence.

Advantages of using PowerPoint

METHOD

I   With slide 2 displayed in **Slide View**, select the word **using** by double-clicking on it.

2   Press: **Delete**.

Information

Other ways of deleting text

Position the cursor to the left of the first character that you want to delete and press: **Delete** until all the text (and the spaces) have been deleted.

or:

Position the cursor to the right of the last character you want to delete and press: ◄— **Del** (backspace) key (top right of main keyboard) until all the text (and the spaces) has been deleted.

or:

Select the text by holding down the left mouse button and dragging the mouse over the text, then releasing the mouse button. Press: **Delete**.

Information

Moving around your text

Moving around your text within placeholders using the arrow keys

The arrow keys ◄— ↑ —► ↓ (located at the bottom right of the main keyboard) allow you to move the cursor (a flashing black vertical line) in the direction of the arrows.

You can move one space forwards or backwards at a time, or you can move up or down one line at a time. If you keep an arrow key pressed down, the cursor will move quickly through the text. Remember to release the arrow key when you reach the required place.

Moving around your text using the mouse
As you move the mouse around the screen, you will notice that the I-beam moves with you. Move it until you have reached the required position, click the left mouse button once and the cursor will appear where you clicked.

Using *Ctrl + Home* and *Ctrl + End*
Hold down: **Ctrl** at the same time as the **Home** key to move to the first slide.
Hold down: **Ctrl** key at the same time as the **End** key to move to the last slide.

Note: If the cursor is positioned in a placeholder, you will move to the beginning/end of the placeholder.

2.3 Using Search and Replace

You may need to replace a word on a particular slide (or throughout) to update or modify the presentation. There is a quick way to do this.

Exercise 3

Replace the word **PowerPoint** with **Software** throughout.

Handy reference

Search and Replace
Edit menu, **Replace**.

METHOD

1 Make sure you do not have any placeholders selected (click in the margins of the slide). From the **Edit** menu, select: **Select All** (see Figure 3.10).
2 From the **Edit** menu, select: **Replace**.
3 The **Replace** dialogue box is displayed (see Figure 3.10).
4 In the **Find what** box, key in: **PowerPoint**.
5 In the **Replace with** box, key in: **Software**.
6 Click on: **Replace All**.
7 Click on: **Close**.

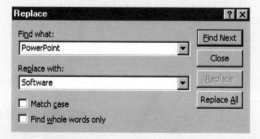

Figure 3.10 *Replace dialogue box*

Information

Replacing text

You can replace phrases as well as single words. Key the phrases into the relevant boxes. If you are looking for specific occurrences of a certain word – e.g. the town **Cardigan** and not the garment **cardigan** – key in the word with a capital first letter. Click on the **Match case** box so that a tick appears.

Note: This applies to text in the **Find what** box. The replacement text should be keyed in exactly as you want it to appear. If you are replacing whole words only, click in the **Find whole words only** box. If you then enter **cardigan**, it will not find **cardigans**.

2.4 Inserting special characters

Sometimes you may want to insert characters other than those on the keyboard – for example, a Greek mathematical symbol Σ, the copyright symbol ©, or an accented character é.

Exercise 4

Insert a special character of your choice on Slide 2 of the presentation.

Handy reference

Inserting special characters
Insert menu,
Symbol.

METHOD

1   Position the cursor on your slide where you want the character to appear.
2   From the **Insert** menu, select: **Symbol**.
3   The **Symbol** dialogue box is displayed (see Figure 3.11). Symbols for the chosen font are displayed. (Select other fonts that contain different symbols from the drop-down list.)
4   Click on the symbol you want.
5   Click on: **Insert**.
6   Click on: **Close**.

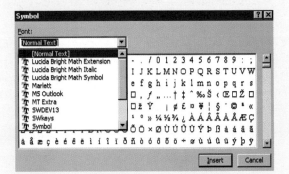

Figure 3.11 *Inserting special characters*

Exercise 5

Run the spellchecker through the presentation.

METHOD

1   Position the cursor on slide 1 of the presentation.
2   Click on: the 🔤 **Spelling** button.
3   The **Spelling** dialogue box is displayed (see Figure 3.12). It will not
     display if you have no errors!

Figure 3.12 *Spelling dialogue box*

The spellchecker will go through your text and match it with the words
in its dictionary. It will highlight unrecognisable words. (You may not have
made any spelling errors!) The dictionary does not contain proper
names, abbreviations, or specific domain language and will treat these as
misspelt words. In the example above, it has highlighted the word **tto**
and it is offering several preferred replacements. Note: It highlights the
one that it thinks is closest to the word you have misspelt. In this case it
is wrong, as it should be the word **to**. To correct:

a   Click on the correct word in the **Suggestions box**.
b   Click on: **Change**.

The spellchecker will repeat this process until it has finished checking
the document. It will then display a message to advise that the spellcheck
is complete.

Information

The *Spelling* dialogue box

There are many options to choose in the **Spelling** dialogue box (see Figure 3.12). The table below shows what these options are.

Option	What it does
Ignore	Click on: **Ignore** if you are happy with the word as it is.
Ignore All	Click on: **Ignore All** if you want each occurrence of the word left as it is.
Change	Click on: **Change** when you have chosen the correct spelling from the list in the **Suggestions** box.
Change All	Click on: **Change All** when you want to change each occurrence of the word.
Add words to CUSTOM.DIC	Words that you use often and that are not included in the main dictionary will display as errors. You can add these words to a custom dictionary by clicking on: **Add**.
Suggest	Click on: **Suggest** to display alternative spellings (if this is not already the default).
Autocorrect	If there is a word that you consistently spell/key in incorrectly, click on: **Autocorrect**. PowerPoint will automatically correct the word after you have keyed it in from then on.
Close	Click on: **Close** to abort the spellcheck at any time.

Note: Spelling in embedded objects such as charts, in special text effects using **WordArt**, or in inserted objects is not checked by the spellchecker.

Remember: Sometimes when you are concentrating on an overall look for a presentation, it is easy to overlook a simple mistake. When producing PowerPoint presentations, it is vitally important that you do not embarrass yourself by having a glaring spelling error. Using the Spellchecker will catch most mistakes but be aware of its limitations. It may not pick up wrong usage of words – for example, where and were, stair and stare. Although these words are spelt correctly it may be that they are being used in the wrong context.

Information

Spellchecker options

You may already have noticed wavy red lines under some words in your presentation. As you key in text, PowerPoint flags up words that it does not recognise. This is because you have the **Check spelling as you type** option turned on. To change this option or view other options from the **Tools** menu, select: **Options**. The **Options** dialogue box appears (see Figure 3.13). With the **Spelling and Style** tab selected, in the **Spelling** section, select any options you want. Click on: **OK**.

Figure 3.13 *Options* *dialogue box*

2.6 Aligning text

Text can be aligned within placeholders. When using **AutoLayouts**, text will align according to the **AutoLayout** default settings. Follow the methods below to realign text.

Aligning text within placeholders

Handy reference

Aligning text within placeholders
Use **Formatting** toolbar buttons.

METHOD

1. Select the text to align.
2. Click on the relevant **Formatting** toolbar button (see Figure 3.14).

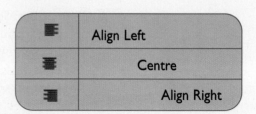

Figure 3.14 *Aligning text*

Changing the size of placeholders

Note: If you enter more text than can fit in the placeholder, PowerPoint will not automatically expand the placeholder to fit the text within it. You could change the font size or alternatively resize the placeholder.

Handy reference

Resizing placeholders
Use the mouse to drag in/out to the required size.

METHOD

1 Select the placeholder by clicking on it.
2 Position the mouse pointer on one of the sizing handles. The pointer changes into a double-headed arrow.
3 Using the left mouse button, drag the border to resize the box (see Figure 3.15).

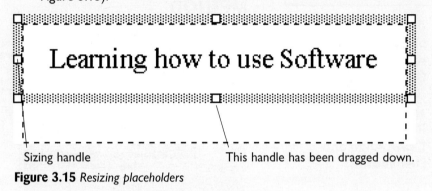

Sizing handle   This handle has been dragged down.

Figure 3.15 *Resizing placeholders*

Moving placeholders

Handy reference

Moving placeholders
Use the *drag and drop* method.

METHOD

1 Select the placeholder by clicking on it.
2 Position the mouse pointer on the placeholder border. The pointer changes into four-way arrow.
3 Using the left mouse button, drag the placeholder to the required position.
4 Release the mouse.

Note: This method of moving objects is known as *drag and drop*.

Copying placeholder and text

METHOD

1   Select the text in the placeholder.
2   Click on the 🗐 **Copy** button.
3   Select the position/slide where you want to copy to.
4   Click on the 🗐 **Paste** button.

Automatically aligning placeholder in relation to the slide

Handy reference

Aligning placeholder in relation to slide Drawing toolbar: click on: **Draw, Align and Distribute, Relative to Slide, Draw, Align and Distribute**.

METHOD

1   Select the placeholder.
2   On the **Drawing** toolbar, click on: **Draw** and then select: **Align or Distribute**.
3   Click on: **Relative to Slide** so that a tick appears.
4   Click on: **Draw** again and select: **Align or Distribute**, then click on the option you want (see Figure 3.16).

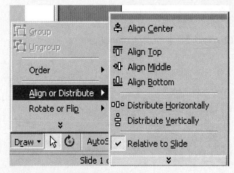

Figure 3.16 *Aligning objects*

Deleting placeholders

Handy reference

Deleting placeholders Edit menu, **Cut**.

METHOD

1   Select the placeholder to delete.
2   From the **Edit** menu, select: **Cut**.

Note: If the placeholder has any content, you will need to repeat step 2 since the first time will delete only the placeholder content.

Information

Aligning elements on a slide

When aligning elements on a slide, you may find it useful to have rulers and guides displayed.

Displaying rulers or guides

1   Right-click on the slide (not in a placeholder).
2   From the pop-up menu, select: **Ruler/Guides**.

Turning off rulers or guides

Repeat steps 1 and 2 above.
(For more information consult the PowerPoint online help.)

2.8 Bullets and numbering

You created a slide with a bulleted list in Chapter 2. Here are some exercises that will help you learn and practise more bullets and numbering skills.

Changing bullet characters

Exercise 6

On slide 2 change the bullet type from ● to ■.

Handy reference

Amending bullets
and numbering
Format menu,
**Bullets and
Numbering**.

METHOD

1   With slide 2 displayed in **Slide View**, select the bulleted list text.
2   From the **Format** menu, select: **Bullets and numbering**.
3   The **Bullets and Numbering** dialogue box is displayed (see Figure 3.17).

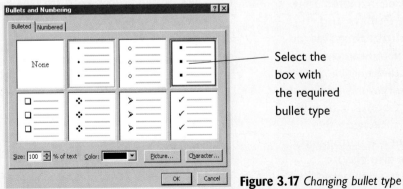

Figure 3.17 *Changing bullet type*

4   Select the box displaying the bullet type required.
5   Click on: **OK**.

Exercise 7

Change the bullet type to ☺.

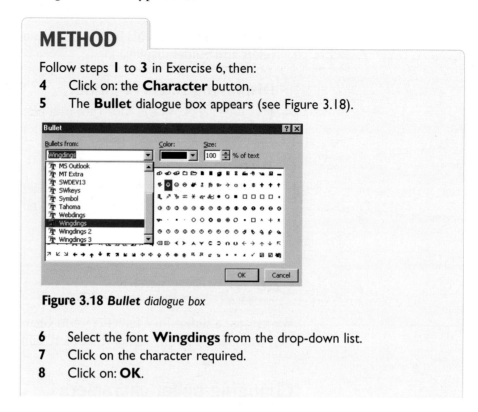
Changing bullets to numbers

Exercise 8

Change the bulleted list to a numbered list.

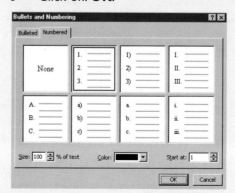

Removing bullets/numbering

You may not always want bulleted text!

METHOD

1 Select the bulleted/numbered list.
2 Click on: the ▤ **Bullets** or ▤ **Numbering** button as appropriate.

Note: You can also create a bulleted/numbered list using these buttons.

(2.9) Multi-level bullets and numbering

Exercise 9

Create a new slide with a bulleted list and enter the following:

Multi-level bulleted list practice
● Côte d'Azur
    – Vieux Nice
    – Promenade des Anglais
    – Le Château
● Antibes
    – Musée Picasso
    – Cours Massena

Handy reference

Bullets: demoting and promoting
Creating a new line with no bullet
Press: **Shift + Enter**.
Promoting paragraphs
Press: **Shift + Tab**
Demoting paragraphs
Press: **Tab**
The promote and demote key combinations also work with text that does not contain bullets. You can also use the **Promote/Demote** toolbar buttons.

METHOD

1 Click on: the **New Slide** button and select: **Bulleted List AutoLayout**.
2 Key in the title text.
3 In the body text placeholder, key in: **Côte d'Azur** and press: **Enter**.
4 To demote the next bullet point, press: the **Tab** key (double-arrow key usually found above the **Caps Lock** key).
5 Key in: **Vieux Nice**, **Promenade des Anglais** and **Le Chateau**, pressing: **Enter** after each.
6 Press: **Shift + Tab** to promote the bullet.
7 Key in: **Antibes**.
8 Repeat steps **4** and **5** using the correct text.

2.10 Line spacing

Changing line spacing

Handy reference

Changing line spacing
Format menu, **Line Spacing**.

METHOD

1   Select the text to change.
2   From the **Format** menu, select: **Line Spacing**.
3   The **Line Spacing** dialogue box is displayed (see Figure 3.20).

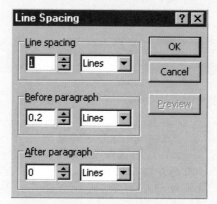

Figure 3.20 *Changing line spacing*

4   Select the spacing required (this can be measured in **Lines** or **Points** units).
5   Click on: **OK**.

Information

The **Formatting** toolbar buttons (see Figure 3.21) are very useful in achieving spacing results.

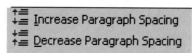

Figure 3.21 Formatting *toolbar buttons*

However, these do not automatically show and need to be added to the toolbar.

Information

Adding/removing toolbar buttons

1   Click on: the **More Buttons** button at the right of the toolbar.
2   Click on: **Add or Remove Buttons** (see Figure 3.22).
3   Select the buttons you want to add/remove by clicking on them.

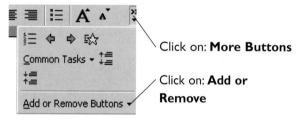

Click on: **More Buttons**

Click on: **Add or Remove**

Figure 3.22 *Add or Remove Buttons*

(2.11) Importing text from another application

Sometimes you will have text already keyed in in another application, such as Word. You can import this text into PowerPoint instead of having to rekey it.

METHOD

1   Open the application and the document containing the text.
2   Select the text.
3   Click on: the **Copy** button (the text is placed on a Clipboard; you will not see or be told this).
4   Close the application.
5   Select the slide and placeholder where you want the text to be placed.
6   Click on: **Paste**.

Information

Copying and Pasting

Using the **Copy** and **Paste** buttons, text and other objects, such as clip art and charts, can be inserted into the presentation.
Sometimes you may have problems with this method and you will need to use the **Insert** menu. Using the **Insert** menu will generally result in a smaller object file size. It is worth considering this if you have limited memory on your computer.

3.1 What is WordArt?

Using the **WordArt** facilities of PowerPoint, you are able to insert imaginative text into your slides. **WordArt** can be used to create things like logos. It is worth noting that PowerPoint does not see **WordArt** as text, but as a **WordArt** object. As such, it is not manipulated in the same way as the text we have looked at in the previous sections. Figure 3.23 shows an example slide containing **WordArt**.

Figure 3.23 *An example of WordArt*

3.2 Accessing WordArt

Exercise 1

Create a new presentation and use **Blank AutoLayout** for slide 1. Using **WordArt** display the following: **WordArt is jazzy**.

Handy reference

Inserting WordArt
Insert menu, **Picture**, **WordArt**.

METHOD

1   Load PowerPoint and create a new presentation. Select **Blank AutoLayout** for slide 1.
2   Change to **Slide View**.
3   From the **Insert** menu, select: **Picture**, then **WordArt** (see Figure 3.24).

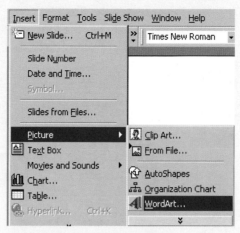

Figure 3.24 *Inserting WordArt*

4 The **WordArt Gallery** is displayed (see Figure 3.25).

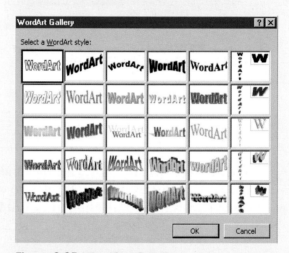

Figure 3.25 *WordArt Gallery*

5 Click on the type of effect you want, then on: **OK**.
6 The **Edit WordArt Text** dialogue box is displayed (see Figure 3.26).

Figure 3.26 *Entering WordArt text*

7 Key in the text in the **Text** box.
Note: You can change the font, size and embolden and italicise in this box.

8 Click on: **OK**.

9 The **WordArt** is inserted on the slide and the **WordArt** toolbar is displayed (see Figure 3.27).

Figure 3.27 *WordArt inserted and WordArt toolbar appears*

3.3 Amending WordArt

The **WordArt** object has sizing handles and a yellow diamond shape that can be used to distort the text. It is fun to experiment and discover what you can do with **WordArt** using the **WordArt** toolbar. It is quite straightforward, so enjoy yourself!

Practise your skills

Load PowerPoint and the presentation file **Sleep** from the CD-ROM. Make the following amendments to the presentation.

1   Slide 1   Replace **ABC Learner** with [**your name**].
2   Spellcheck the presentation.
3   Slide 2   Insert the word **more** between **skin is** and **porous**.
4   Slide 5   Centre horizontally the body text starting **We are approximately** … within the placeholder and in relation to the slide.
5   Change the line spacing of the above paragraph to **44 point**.
6   Slide 4   Add to the bulleted list after **Slows down** as follows:
      ● **Slows down**
        – **Not moving around**
        – **Sleep slows speed at which we carry out bodily functions**
7   Slide 4   Add the following notes:
      Weight training – the more muscle you have, the more calories you burn.
8   Slide 3   Add the following notes:
      Mites can't survive in humidity of less than 50%.
9   Create a new slide at the end of the presentation. Insert (using **WordArt**) the words: **While we sleep**. Format the **WordArt** as you wish, but centre it to fill most of the slide.
10 Copy the **WordArt** in step **9** to slide **1**. Decrease its size so that it fits at the bottom right-hand corner and change its colours from the default.
11 Replace the word: **truth** with the word: **facts** wherever it occurs.
12 Slides   Change font type of all of the titles to sans serif 40 pt
     2 to 5   bold, colour dark green. (**Hint**: Use **Format Painter** or
     inclusive   **Format** menu, **Replace Fonts**.)
13 Slide 5   Change round bullets ● to ☐ shapes.
14 Slide 1   Change the case of the title to upper case.
15 Slide 1   Change the text: **What happens when we sleep?** to: **What happens when we are asleep?**
16 Create a new blank slide at the end of the presentation. Copy your name from slide **1** to this new slide.
17 Insert the text: **Eliminate dust mites – foam pillows, anti-mite spray, anti-allergy bedding** from the Word file **Dust Mites** on the CD-ROM so that it appears with the notes on Slide 3.
18 Slide 2   Insert the word: **more** between **reactions** and **likely**.
19 Slide 2   Delete the word: **now**.

20   Create a new slide with the title: **Joints – the facts** followed by a multi-level bulleted list:

- **Joint pain is worse at night**
- **Osteoarthritis sufferers**
  - **Worse on getting into bed**
- **Rheumatoid arthritis**
  - **Worse in the early hours**

21   Save the presentation file with the file name: **Sleep[your initials]**.

22   Print the file, one slide per page.

23   Close the file and exit PowerPoint.

Chapter 4 Master slides, templates, organising slides

Introduction

This chapter introduces working with master slides and templates. It is quite difficult to understand the relationships and concepts of **Master Slides** and **Templates**. However, it is well worth spending time on this now since it will save you time in the long run.

There are also instructions for organising slides, including copying slides from other presentations.

Master Slides

There are four master slides and this book covers **Slide Master** and **Title Master** in detail. The audience never sees master slides. They are for your use in designing the presentation. The **Handouts** and **Notes Masters** are usually acceptable in their default forms.

Slide Master	Use this to set up all slides.
Title Master	Use this if you want the **Title Slide(s)** to differ from other slides in the presentation.
Handouts Master	Use this for creating customised **Handouts**.
Notes Master	Use this for creating customised **Notes pages**.

As mentioned in Chapter 2, PowerPoint bases all of its slides on **AutoLayouts**. The **AutoLayout** text formatting, positioning of placeholders, colour scheme and so on are automatically based on the master slide defaults. In previous chapters we have not changed these default settings. However, it is a good idea to set up customised master slides because this ensures that all of the slides in the presentation contain the common elements you have chosen, as well as consistent formatting to suit your needs. This results in a more cohesive presentation. Once the elements, such as logo, date and so on, have been inserted on the master slides, they will automatically appear on all slides in the presentation unless you change them. You can change the master slide's layout at any time.

The **Slide Master** is used to set up all slides in the presentation. Any changes from the defaults or any additions to the **Slide Master** will automatically appear on other slides in the presentation.

The **Title Slide AutoLayout** differs from other slides in the presentation in that it can have a different look if you want it to. If not, it will take on the look of the **Slide Master**. This **AutoLayout** is provided to be the first slide in a presentation or to separate sections. Therefore you may not require all of the elements or the same colour scheme for such slides.

Note: You can have more than one **Title Slide** in a presentation. There is a **Title Master** slide which enables you to customise only the **Title Slide AutoLayout**.

Templates

To save you having to do all the design work on your slides, PowerPoint provides templates that have been professionally designed. These are called **Design Templates**. When you apply a **Design Template** to a presentation, it places the design on all slides in the presentation since it applies the design to the master slides. You can still change the master slides and so create and save your own designs as templates for future use.

If you are going to use **Design Templates** and set up **Master Slides**, this is best done in the following order:

1 Apply **Design Template**.
2 Set up **Slide Master**.
3 Set up **Title Master** (if you want it to be different from **Slide Master**).
4 Enter text and objects into individual slides.

Title AutoLayout

The **Title AutoLayout** slide is the only slide that allows a non-bulleted text entry placeholder under the Title text placeholder. Many people use this **AutoLayout** for this reason. Ideally, it is best to use the **Title AutoLayout** for beginnings of sections only, since you may want to format it differently to other slides in the presentation. (You have already learnt how easy it is to remove bullets from other slide **AutoLayouts** in **Chapter 3**.)

Learning objectives

- Access master slides
- Customise **Slide Master**
- Change slide background

- Add a text box
- Customise **Title Master**

1.1 Accessing Master Slides

Exercise 1

Open a new presentation. Customise the **Slide Master** for this presentation.

Handy reference

Accessing Slide Master
View menu, **Master**, **Slide Master**.

METHOD

1 Load PowerPoint and a new presentation, selecting **Bulleted List AutoLayout** for slide 1.
  Note: Any **AutoLayout** slide can be selected at this stage but preferably not **Blank AutoLayout** (since you will not see the effect of the formatting within placeholders).

2 From the **View** menu, select: **Master**, **Slide Master** (see Figure 4.1).

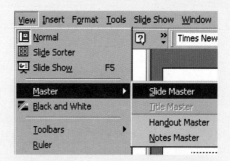

Figure 4.1 *Accessing the Slide Master*

The **Slide Master** is displayed (see Figure 4.2). Notice that the different areas are labelled: **Title Area; Object Area** (this has five body text levels and can hold text, bulleted lists, charts, pictures and so on); **Date Area; Footer Area; Number Area.**

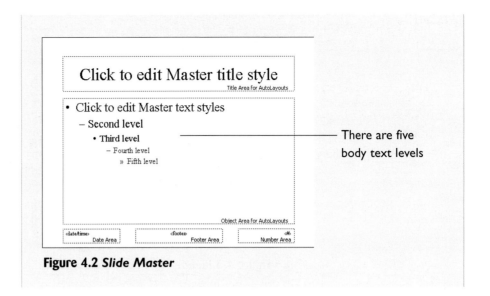

Figure 4.2 *Slide Master*

Exercise 2

Customise the **Slide Master** to suit your presentation.

METHOD

It is up to you how you change the **Slide Master**. Here are some suggestions that you can practise:

- Change the sizes and positions of the placeholders.
- Change the font, colour and sizes.
- Change the bullet type.
- Change the bullets to numbers.
- Delete the bullets.
- Add colours to bullets/numbers.
- Change the line spacing.
- Add the date, a footer and slide number.
- Change the slide background.

I   You have already learnt how to do the first seven of these so you could do those first.

Adding date, footer and slide number

2   From the **View** menu, select: **Header and Footer**.
3   The **Header and Footer** dialogue box is displayed (see Figure 4.3).

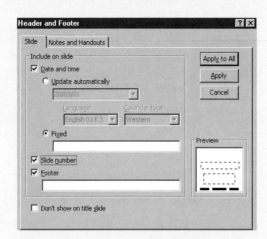

Figure 4.3 *Header and Footer dialogue box*

Hint

You can also delete placeholders that you are not using from the **Slide Master** by selecting the placeholder and pressing: **Delete**.
To restore placeholders
Right-click on the slide and select the placeholder to reinstate.

4 With the **Slide** tab selected, use the check boxes to determine what to include on your slides. If using **Date and time**, select whether you want this to be **Updated automatically** (to display the current date), or **Fixed** (always using a particular date). If you have chosen **Update automatically**, select the format of the date from the drop-down list. If using **Fixed**, key in the date required. If using **Footer** text, key the text into the box under **Footer**.

Note: You can choose not to show these elements on **Title Slides** by clicking on **Don't show on title slide**. You can also overwrite text in the **Footer** boxes or move the **Footer** boxes to the top of the slide to become **Headers**.

Your **Slide Master** could look something like Figure 4.4.

Note: In case you are beginning to get worried about the array of styles, please note that I would not suggest that this would be a suitable layout for any presentation! It is for practice purposes only.

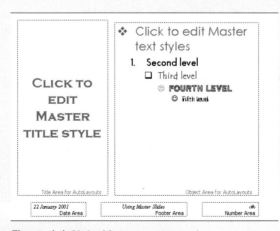

Figure 4.4 *Slide Master customised*

Checking for visual clarity

PowerPoint contains a **Visual Clarity** check facility. You can explore this by selecting: **Options** from the **Tools** menu, **Spelling and Style** tab, **Style Options**, **Visual Clarity** tab.

1.3 Changing the slide background

METHOD

1   From the **Format** menu, select: **Background**.
2   The **Background** dialogue box is displayed (see Figure 4.5).

Figure 4.5 *Changing the slide* **Background**

Changing the background colour

METHOD

1   Select a colour from the drop-down list.
2   Click on: **Apply**.

Note: If you do not see a colour you like, select: **More Colors** and click on a colour on the colour palette.

If selecting a picture background, make sure that it enhances the presentation.

METHOD

1   Return to the **Format** menu, select: **Background**.
2   Experiment with **Fill Effects** by selecting: **Fill Effects** from the drop-down list.
3   By selecting the **Picture** tab (see Figure 4.6), you can choose a relevant picture background (there are several of these to choose from on the CD-ROM in the **Photos and ClipArt** folder/**Backgrounds**).

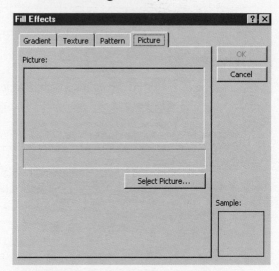

Figure 4.6 *Selecting a **Picture** background*

4   Click on: **Select Picture**.
5   Select the location of the picture.
6   Click on: the picture's file name.
7   Click on: **Insert**.
8   Click on: **OK**.
9   Click on: **Apply/Apply to All** as appropriate.

Information

Colour schemes

Using the **Format** menu and selecting: **Slide Color Scheme**, the **Color Scheme** dialogue box is displayed (see Figure 4.7). From here you can select a **Standard Color scheme** or, by clicking on the **Custom** tab, you can define your own colour scheme. Click on: **Apply** when you are happy with the scheme. Backgrounds should be light for overhead transparencies and handouts and darker for slide shows.

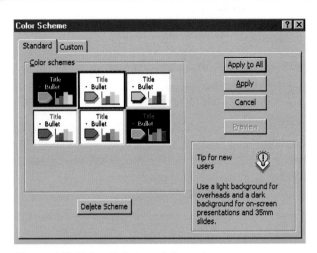

Figure 4.7 *Color Scheme* dialogue box

Information

Changing the colour of individual placeholders

You can also change the colours of individual placeholders. To do this:

1   Select a placeholder.
2   From the **Format** menu, select: **Placeholder**.
3   The **Format AutoShape** dialogue box is displayed (see Figure 4.8).

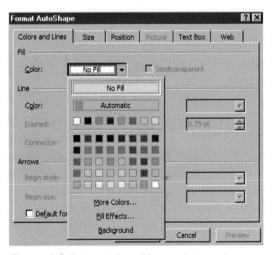

Figure 4.8 *Format AutoShape* dialogue box

4   In the **Fill** section, click on the down arrow of the **Color** box to reveal a drop-down menu.
5   Select a colour and then click on: **OK**.

Note: You can also select: **Fill Effects**. These can be quite interesting and effective.

> **Hint**
>
> As an alternative to using the menu bar, you can right-click over an object to access a relevant pop-up menu.

Exercise 3

View the first slide in the presentation in **Slide View** to see what effect your customised **Slide Master** has on it. Create two more slides so that there are three slides in the presentation. Add text of your choice. Save the presentation.

1.4 Adding a text box to the Slide Master

Exercise 4

Add a text box with your name to the **Slide Master**. Format as you like.

METHOD

1 Display the **Slide Master** in **Slide View**.
2 Use the **Drawing** toolbar, **Text Box** button and enter your name (see **Chapter 2**).
3 Format the text.

(Refer to **Chapter 5** and **Chapter 8** for details on how to insert other objects, such as clip art and logos.)

1.5 Customising the Title Master

Exercise 5

Add a **Title Slide AutoLayout** to your presentation and access and customise the **Title Master**.

Handy reference

Accessing Title Master
View menu, **Master**, **Title Master**.

METHOD

1 Add a **Title Slide AutoLayout** so that it is displayed in **Slide View**.
2 From the **View** menu, select: **Master, Title Master**.

Hint

If the **Title Master** option is greyed out, display the **Slide Master** and then click on: the ▣ **New Slide** button. Access master slides by holding down **Ctrl** at the same time as clicking on the **Slide View** button.

3   The **Title Master** will be displayed.

4   Customise the **Title Master** using the same methods as for the **Slide Master**.

Now look at the effect this has had on the presentation.

Information

Changing an existing slide to a different AutoLayout

You can change an existing slide to a different **AutoLayout** – e.g. change to **Title Slide** layout, so that it will have different attributes. Right-click on the slide, select: **Slide Layout**. Click on the layout you want then on: **Apply**.

Exercise 6

Save the presentation.

Learning objectives

- Apply a design template
- Create a design template

- **AutoContent Wizard**

2.1 Applying Design Templates

Exercise 1

Apply a **Design Template** to a presentation created in a previous section.

Handy reference

Applying Design Templates
Format menu, **Apply Design Template**.

METHOD

1   With the presentation on screen in **Slide View**, from the **Format** menu, select: **Apply Design Template**.
2   The **Apply Design Template** dialogue box is displayed (see Figure 4.9).

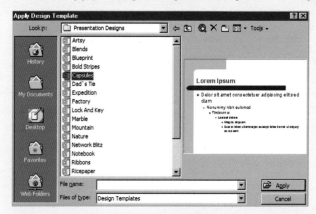

Figure 4.9 *Applying a **Design Template***

3   There are many designs to choose from. Click once on a design to see a preview of it on the right.
4   Double-click on the design you want for it to be implemented on your presentation.

Note: The new design overwrites the master slides' formatting and other elements. However, you are still able to access the master slides and customise them as you want. The new design does not overwrite any formatting or changes that you have made to individual slides. However, if you do want to overwrite these, from the **Format** menu, select: **Slide Layout**. The **Slide Layout** dialogue box is displayed. Select the **AutoLayout** (if not already selected). Click on: **Reapply**.

Hint

There are more **Design Templates** in the **Templates, 1033** folder. This can be accessed by clicking on the down-arrow in the **Look in** box. Click on **Templates**, then double-click on: **1033**.

Quick change Design Template colours

You can quickly change the design template colours by using the **Format** menu, **Slide Color Scheme** and selecting one of the **Standard** colour schemes.

Practise adding other design templates and altering the master slides.

2.2 Creating your own design template

You can save your presentation design (whether designed from scratch or adapted from an existing design template) as a design template.

Saving a Design Template

METHOD

1   With your presentation displayed, from the **File** menu, select: **Save As**.
2   The **Save As** dialogue box is displayed (see Figure 4.10).

Figure 4.10 *Saving a Design Template*

3   Select where you want to save the new **Design Template**.
4   In the **File** name box, key in the file name.
5   Click on the down arrow in the **Save as type** box and select: **Design Template** from the drop-down list.
6   Click on: **Save**.

Accessing Design Template

If the **Design Template** is saved in the **Templates** folder, to access it *either*:

1   From the **PowerPoint** dialogue box that is displayed on loading PowerPoint, click in the **Design Template** option button and then on: **OK**.
2   The **New Presentation** dialogue box is displayed.
3   Select the **General** tab, then double-click on the template file.

or:

1   From the **File** menu, select: **New**.
2   Follow steps **2** and **3** above.

If the **Design Template** is saved elsewhere, at step **3**, with the **General** tab selected, right-click in the white area and select: **Explore** from the pop-up menu. Locate the **Design Template** and double-click on it.

2.3   Using the AutoContent Wizard

You may find it interesting to look at creating a presentation using the **AutoContent Wizard**. There are several topic-specific pre-formatted layouts and suggested content presentations that can be accessed using the **AutoContent Wizard**. You follow the wizard's instructions to produce such presentations.

Hint

You can also access these pre-formatted and content presentations by selecting the **Presentations** tab in the **New Presentation** dialogue box.

METHOD

1   From the PowerPoint dialogue box, which is displayed on loading PowerPoint, click in the **AutoContent Wizard** option button and then on: **OK**.
2   Follow the on-screen instructions.

or

1   From the **File** menu, select: **New**.
2   The **New Presentation** dialogue box is displayed.
3   Select the **General** tab, then double-click on the **AutoContent Wizard** file.

Figure 4.11 shows an example of a presentation produced using the
AutoContent Wizard.

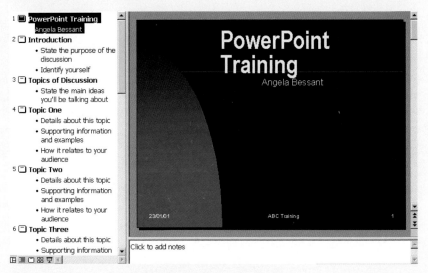

Figure 4.11 *Example of an* **AutoContent** *presentation*

Learning objectives

- Delete slides
- Reorder slides
- Insert a new slide within a presentation

- Copy slides from other presentations
- Change slide orientation

This section shows how to manage slides within presentations. You will need to access two files on the CD-ROM – **Insurance and Motor** – to complete the exercises.

3.1 Deleting slides

Exercise 1

Load PowerPoint and the presentation file **Insurance**. Delete slide 2 of this presentation.

METHOD

1 Load PowerPoint and the relevant presentation.
2 Save the file on your own computer.
3 Change to **Slide Sorter View**.
4 Click on **Slide 2** to select it (see Figure 4.12).

Figure 4.12 *Slide 2 selected in **Slide Sorter View***

5 Press: **Delete**.

Exercise 2

Move slide 3, containing the text: **For a free quote** ... so that it becomes the last slide in the presentation.

METHOD

In **Slide Sorter View,** hold down the left mouse button on Slide 3 and drag to the required position.

Exercise 3

Insert a new slide that will become the second slide in the presentation. Enter the following text on this new slide.

What can Carlton offer?
1. Great value for money
2. Dependable response

METHOD

1 In **Slide Sorter View,** click in between the slides where the new slide will be positioned – between slide 1 and slide 2 (see Figure 4.13).

Figure 4.13 *Inserting a new slide*

2 Click on the: **New Slide** button.
3 Select an appropriate **AutoLayout**.
4 Change to **Slide View**.
5 Enter the text.

Sometimes you may be creating a presentation that communicates information you have already used on slides in a previously prepared presentation. It will save time and effort if you copy the relevant slide(s) to your current presentation. If you have created a **Master Slide(s)** for the current presentation, the copied slide(s) will automatically reformat to take on the properties of the current presentation.

Exercise 4

Copy slides 2 and 3 from the presentation file **Motor** so that they become the last two slides in the presentation file **Insurance** that you are working on.

METHOD

1   Copy the relevant file to your computer.
2   In **Slide Sorter View**, click where you want the copied slides to be – after the last slide (6).
3   From the **Insert** menu select: **Slides from Files**. The **Slide Finder** dialogue box is displayed (see Figure 4.14).

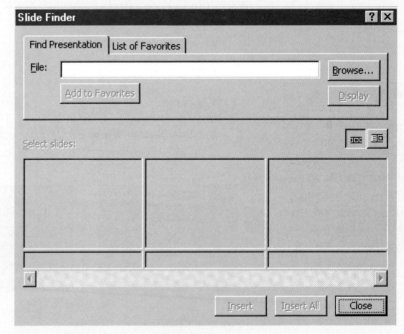

Figure 4.14 *Slide Finder* dialogue box

4   With the **Find Presentation** tab selected, click on: **Browse** to locate the presentation **Motor** containing the slides to copy.
5   Double-click on: the PowerPoint file name.

6 The first few slides will be displayed in the **Select slides** section (see Figure 4.15).

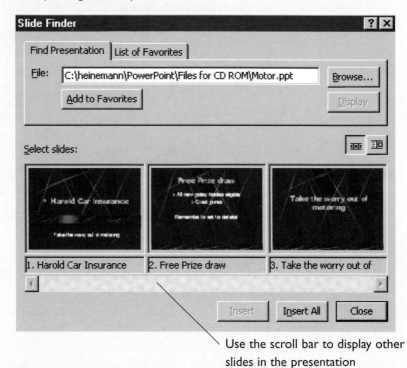

Use the scroll bar to display other slides in the presentation

Figure 4.15 *Slides are displayed*

Hint

Copy all the slides you want to use to the same place in the presentation. Then reorganise them later in **Slide Sorter View**.

7 Select the slides to copy (2 and 3) by clicking on them while holding down the **Ctrl** key. "To deselect a slide, click on it again. Use the scroll bar to access further slides in the presentation."

8 Click on: **Insert**.

9 The slides are inserted into the current presentation.

10 When you have finished inserting the slides you require, click on: **Close** to close the **Slide Finder** dialogue box.

3.5 Changing slide orientation

Exercise 5

Change the orientation of the slides in the presentation you are working on to **Portrait** display.

METHOD

1   From the **File** menu, select: **Page Setup**.
2   The **Page Setup** dialogue box is displayed (see Figure 4.16).

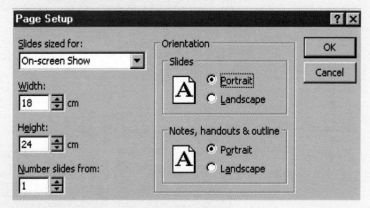

Figure 4.16 *Orientation of slides*

3   In the **Orientation**, **Slides** section, click in the **Portrait** option button.
4   Click on: **OK**.

Exercise 6

Save and print all the slides in the current presentation. Change the orientation back to **Landscape** and resave. Close the file and exit PowerPoint.

Practise your skills

1   Create a new PowerPoint presentation with the following content:

Slide Number	Content
1	THE CAPPUCCINO SHOP A progressive company
2	BEGINNINGS ● Opened first shop in 1996 ● Two founding members ● Expertise is catering management
3	NOW ● Shop number 25 opened last week ● More than 100 permanent staff ● More than 50 temporary staff ● Turnover last year in excess of £1 million
4	FUTURE PLANS ● Expand in the UK ● Open shops in Australia and the US ● Develop a new branch – PANCAKE SHOP

2   Apply a suitable **Design Template**.
3   Adjust the **Master Slide** as follows:

Component	Input	Other information
Background	Change colour from original on chosen **Design Template**	Ensure the text is still legible against the new background colour
Date	10 February 2002	Default font
Slide numbering	Insert slide numbers on all slides	Default font
Footer	Insert your name	Default font
Company name	Insert a text box with the text THE CAPPUCCINO SHOP at the top left	Sans serif, bold, 14 pt

Text styles:

Style	Font	Size	Emphasis	Alignment
Heading	Sans serif	44–60	Bold	Centre
Sub-heading	Sans serif	28–34	Default	Centre
Bullet	Sans serif	18–26	Italic	Left

4   Reorder the slides so that slide 2 becomes the last slide.
5   Insert a new slide after slide 1 as follows:
    WHAT DO WE DO?
    ● **Provide delicious beverages and snacks**
    ● **All snacks are baked on the premises daily**
    ● **Fresh seasonal ingredients**
6   Insert a slide between slides 3 and 4 from an existing presentation (of your choice).
7   Save and print the presentation as handouts (six per page).

Chapter 5 Graphics, sound and animation

Introduction

In this chapter you will learn how to use the Drawing toolbar to add different types of lines, shapes and free-drawn objects to your slides. These skills also enable you to format text boxes and other objects. You will be introduced to clip art (ready-made artwork) and will learn how to add it to your slides and how to manage it once it is there. Inserting photographs into slides is also covered together with inserting animated clips (moving diagrams or cartoons) and sound.

There is an abundance of media clips available and adding specially selected material can reinforce your message and make your presentation more lively and interesting. However, you may not always find the perfect image, sound, etc. that you require. In such cases do not be tempted to use something that is not quite appropriate. Most likely it will not enhance your presentation and would probably detract attention from your message. It cannot be stressed enough that you must be wary of overusing your newfound skills! Always ask yourself if the media element is working to good effect. If in doubt, err on the cautious side and do not use it. Always remember that it is your message you need to communicate and not your PowerPoint skills. That said, it is great fun to explore and experiment with the endless possibilities. Enjoy!

1   Using the Drawing toolbar

Learning objectives

● Add lines and shapes

● Set line weights, styles and colours

1.1   Adding lines and shapes

Exercise 1

Open a new presentation and a blank slide. Use this slide to practise adding lines and shapes.

METHOD

1   Open a new PowerPoint presentation.
2   Click on: the **New Slide** button.
3   Select: **Blank AutoLayout**.
4   Ensure you are in **Slide View** with the **Drawing** toolbar visible. If not, from the **View** menu, select: **Toolbars, Drawing** so that a tick appears next to it. The **Drawing** toolbar is shown in Figure 5.1.

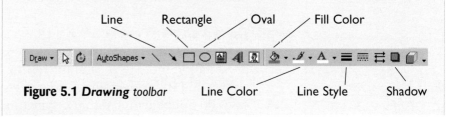

Figure 5.1 Drawing toolbar

Adding a line

Hint

Hold down the **Shift** key when creating lines, squares, etc. for a perfectly straight line, square, circle or other object.

METHOD

1   Click on: the **Line** button.
2   Position the crosshair where you want the line to start.
3   Hold down the left mouse button and drag the mouse to where you want the line to end. Release the mouse.

Formatting the line

METHOD

1   Select the line by clicking on it. When it is selected, handles appear at each end.
2   Click on: the **Line Style** button.
3   Click on the line style that you want.
4   Click on the down-arrow of the **Line Color** button to choose the line colour.

Changing line length and moving a line

METHOD

1   Click on the line to select it.
2   Change the length by dragging the handles to the required length.
3   Move the line by holding down the left mouse button anywhere along its length until the arrowhead cross appears and then dragging it to the new position.
4   Release the mouse button.

Copying a line or other drawn object

METHOD

1   Click on the line to select it.
2   Right-click on the line.
3   Select: **Copy**.
4   Right-click again.
5   Select: **Paste**.
6   Move the line to where you want it to be.

Adding a circle or ellipse

METHOD

1   Click on: the **Oval** button.
2   Hold down the left mouse button and drag out to the required shape.
3   Release the mouse button.

Adding a rectangle

METHOD

Follow the method for a circle/ellipse, shown above, but clicking on: the **Rectangle** button.

Filling an object with colour

METHOD

1   Select the object to fill.
2   Click on: the **Fill Color** button.
3   Click on the chosen colour.

Filling a shape with a pattern

METHOD

Follow steps 1 and 2 above.
3   Click on: **Fill Effects**. The **Fill Effects** dialogue box appears.
4   Click on: the **Pattern** tab.
5   Click on the chosen pattern. Click on: **OK**.

Applying a shadow

METHOD

1   Select the required object.
2   Click on: the **Shadow** button.

Adding AutoShapes

METHOD

Click on: the **AutoShapes** button. Select from the menu. This includes many useful shapes and lines, including **Callouts** (boxes where you can enter your own text), arrows and basic shapes.

Adding free-drawn lines

METHOD

1   Click on: the **AutoShapes** button.
2   Select: **Lines**, **Freeform** or **Scribble** (see Figure 5.2).

Figure 5.2 *Free-drawn lines*

3   Hold down the left mouse and draw with the 'pencil'.
4   Double-click to finish.

Note: Check the other options on this menu – they may be very useful.

Rotating or flipping an object

METHOD

1   Select the object.
2   Click on: the **Draw** button, select: **Rotate** or **Flip** and then select from the next menu (see Figure 5.3).

Figure 5.3 *Rotating and flipping objects*

Information

Grouping/ungrouping

Objects can be grouped so that they stay together and you will then be able to reposition them as a group instead of as individual components. To do this: hold down **Shift** and click in turn on the objects to group. From the **Drawing** toolbar, **Draw** menu, select: **Group**. (**Ungroup** from this menu to edit individual components.) Experiment with other **Drawing** toolbar buttons to create some stunning effects.

Ordering

When drawn objects overlap, you can set the order in which they are layered on the slide by right-clicking on an object, selecting: **Order** from the pop-up menu and then selecting from the menu (see Figure 5.4). This allows you to, for example, add colour-filled shapes behind text for extra impact.

Figure 5.4 *Layering*

1.2 Setting line weights, styles and colours in text boxes

Exercise 2

Create a text box at the top of the slide. Insert the text: **Adding shapes and lines**. Format the text box.

METHOD

1   Add a text box in the same way as other objects (see **Chapter 2**) and key in the text.
2   With the text box selected, format it using the **Drawing** toolbar buttons.

2 ▸ Working with ClipArt

Learning objectives

- Insert ClipArt
  - Resize ClipArt
  - About the **Clip Gallery**
- Change ClipArt colours
- Insert animated ClipArt and sounds
- Access more ClipArt, media clips
- Insert other pictures
  - Crop a picture

2.1 ▸ Inserting ClipArt

Exercise 1

Open a new or existing presentation and add a piece of ClipArt to a new slide.

Handy reference

Inserting ClipArt
Double-click in the **Clip Art** placeholder.
or
Insert menu, **Picture**, **Clip Art**.

METHOD

1 With the presentation in **Slide View**, click on the 🖼 **New Slide** button.
2 Select the **Text and Clip Art AutoLayout**.
3 Double-click in the ClipArt placeholder.
4 The **Microsoft Clip Gallery** box is displayed (see Figure 5.5).

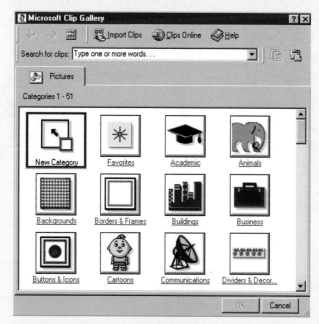

Figure 5.5 *Microsoft Clip Gallery*

5   Select a **Category** by double-clicking on it. The ClipArt for that category is displayed. (You can key in search word(s) in the **Search for clips** box if you prefer.)

6   Select the ClipArt you want to use by right-clicking on it and selecting: **Insert** from the pop-up menu (see Figure 5.6).

Note: If you do not find a suitable piece of ClipArt, click on: the ⏎ **Back** button to return to the categories and try another category.

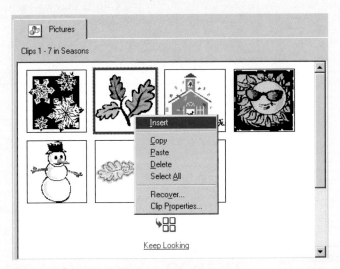

Figure 5.6 *Inserting ClipArt*

7   The clip art appears on your slide and fits into the ClipArt placeholder (see Figure 5.7).

Figure 5.7 *ClipArt inserted into placeholder*

Information

About the Microsoft Clip Gallery

The **Clip Gallery** that is shared with other Office applications contains ClipArt, sound and animated clips. You can also add your own creations to the **Clip Gallery**. You probably did not install all of the clips available on the Office CD-ROM so, in order to access these clips, you will need to insert the MS Office 2000 CD-ROM into the drive before accessing the **Clip Gallery**. If you are connected to the Internet, further clips are available by clicking on **Clips Online** in the Microsoft **Clip Gallery** box which will take you to the **Clip Gallery Live** website.

Adding to the Clip Gallery

1   Select the picture to add to the gallery.
2   From the **Edit** menu, select: **Copy**.
3   On the **Drawing** toolbar, click on: the **Insert ClipArt** button
4   Select the category you want to add it to.
5   Right-click.
6   Select: **Paste** from the pop-up menu.
7   Enter details in the **Clip Properties** box.
8   Click on: **OK**.

2.2   Changing ClipArt colours

You might find a perfect piece of ClipArt whose colours are not right for your particular presentation. It is usually possible to change the colours of the ClipArt.

Exercise 2

Change the colours of the inserted ClipArt.

Hint

To regroup, right-click an object and select: **Regroup**.

METHOD

1   Select the ClipArt so that it displays its handles.
2   Right-click on the ClipArt and select: **Grouping** from the pop-up menu.
3   Select: **Ungroup** (see Figure 5.8).

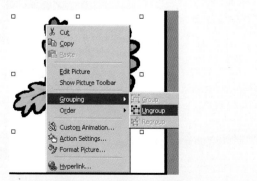

Figure 5.8 *Altering ClipArt properties*

4 A message will be displayed (see Figure 5.9). Click on: **Yes**.

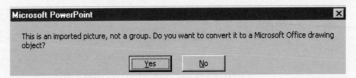

Figure 5.9 *Converting ClipArt to a drawing object*

5 Your ClipArt should now display lots of handles (see Figure 5.10).

Figure 5.10 *ClipArt is now a drawing object*

6 Click in a space to remove the handles.
7 You can now select individual parts of the ClipArt – e.g. one leaf (see Figure 5.11).

Figure 5.11 *Selecting an individual part of the ClipArt*

8 Right-click on the selected part so that a pop-up menu is displayed (see Figure 5.12).
9 Select: **Format AutoShape**.

Figure 5.12 *Formatting the selection*

10 The **Format AutoShape** dialogue box is displayed.
11 With the **Colors and Lines** tab selected, in the **Fill** section, click on the down arrow next to the **Color** box (see Figure 5.13).
12 Click on the required colour and then on: **OK**.
13 Repeat the above for other sections of the ClipArt.

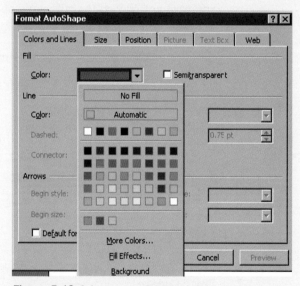

Figure 5.13 *Selecting a colour*

Information

Format AutoShape dialogue box

The **Format AutoShape** dialogue box also allows you to make other alterations, such as **Fill effects**, **Line colours** and so on. It is worth taking time to explore the possibilities.

Dragging the handles of a selection can alter the shapes of different sections of the ClipArt. They can also be deleted by pressing: **Delete**.

As well as inserting static ClipArt you can insert animated (moving) ClipArt and sound from the **Microsoft Clip Gallery**.

Exercise 3

Insert an animated clip or sound clip into a slide.

Hint

Accessing more sound clips
There are lots of sound clips in the **Windows/Media** folder.

METHOD

1 With the slide displayed in **Slide View**, from the **Insert** menu, select: **Movies and Sounds/Movie from Gallery** or **Sound from Gallery**.
2 In the **Search for clips** box, key in the category you want to find clips of.
3 Select what you want to use by right-clicking on it and selecting: **Insert** from the pop-up menu.
4 To view/hear the effect, change to **Slide Show View**. Use the **Page Up** and **Page Down** keys to navigate through your slides. If you have not chosen the automatic option you will need to click on the relevant icon to run the clip, for example:

Inserting media clips

You can also use an **AutoLayout** containing a media clip placeholder.

Deleting sound, media clips

METHOD

1 Select the object (if a sound, the speaker icon).
2 Press: **Delete**.

You may find that you do not have a suitable piece of ClipArt or media clip to suit your needs. Try the following sources:

●   Access more ClipArt on the Internet:

Hint

Be aware of copyright issues when using pictures or sounds. Always check if you need copyright clearance before using them in your work.

METHOD

1   From the **Insert** menu, select: **Picture**, **ClipArt**.
2   Click on **Clips Online** (see Figure 5.14).
3   Follow the instructions on the website.

Figure 5.14 *Accessing more PowerPoint ClipArt*

● Use an Internet search engine such as **www.ask.co.uk**, and key in the question – for example, **Where can I find ClipArt?**
● Specialised software packages.
● Free with computer magazines.

2.5 Inserting other pictures

You can insert pictures and media clips (if you have them) other than those supplied by PowerPoint – for example, those on the CD-ROM, photographs, company logo – into your slide using the **Insert** menu.

METHOD

1   From the **Insert** menu, select: **Picture**, **From File**.
2   Select the file's location.
3   Click once on the file name to see a preview.
4   Click on: **Insert**.

Using the Picture toolbar

You can manipulate your picture in all sorts of ways using the **Picture** toolbar buttons. From the **View** menu, select **Toolbars**, **Picture** (see Figure 5.15). Try these now.

Hint

Watermark
Changing a relevant photograph to a watermark and using it as a background can be very effective.

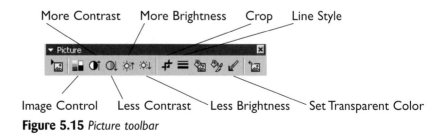

Figure 5.15 *Picture toolbar*

The **Image Control** button gives the following choices (see Figure 5.16):

Figure 5.16 *Image Control* options

Cropping a picture

METHOD

1 Select the image.
2 Click on: the **Crop** button.
3 Position the cursor over one of the picture's handles and it changes to look like that in Figure 5.17.
4 Drag to the required position.

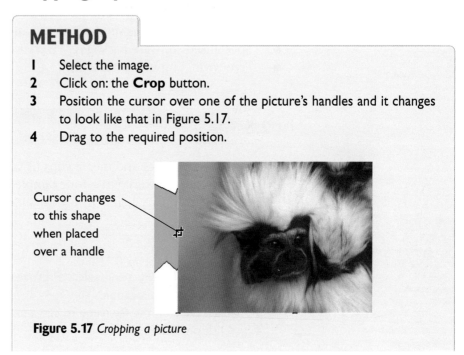

Cursor changes to this shape when placed over a handle

Figure 5.17 *Cropping a picture*

Line Style

The **Line Style** button gives several choices of borders for the picture.

The PowerPoint file **Picture toolbar** on the CD-ROM contains examples of manipulated pictures.

Note: Chapter 8 gives more information on capturing and manipulating your own individual images.

Practise your skills

1   Load PowerPoint and open the presentation file **Sleep** (from the CD-ROM).
2   Add a suitable ClipArt to one of the slides. Change the ClipArt colours to suit the mood of the text on the slide and resize it to fit.
3   Create a new slide to be the last slide in the presentation. Use the **Drawing** toolbar buttons to create a suitable drawn object of your choice.
4   Save the amended file.

Chapter 6 Presenting charts and tables

Introduction

PowerPoint provides quick routes to inserting charts into slides. These can be **Organisational** or **Data** charts.

This chapter will address how to insert organisational charts using the utility application **Microsoft® Organization Chart**, provided in PowerPoint, and how to amend, format and manage them. An organisational chart consists of a number of boxes where you can enter text. The boxes are joined by lines to demonstrate how they relate to one another. They can be used for presenting things such as relationships, sequences of events, company personnel organisations. The organisational charts that you can create using this method tend to be rather restrictive and do not conform to the overall presentation formatting, such as colour scheme and font type. This needs to be amended to suit. However, it is a good method for producing simple charts. For more complex charts you may find it better to use the **Drawing Tools** (see **Chapter 5, Section 1.1**) and text boxes.

Data charts are used for displaying numerical data that could otherwise be difficult to interpret. If you know how to use **Microsoft® Excel** you can create your chart in Excel and insert it as an object into the relevant slide using the **Edit** menu, **Copy** and **Paste** method. This chapter demonstrates how to insert a data chart using the utility application **Microsoft® Graph**, provided in PowerPoint. It then addresses how to edit and amend the chart. The PowerPoint file **Numerical data** on the CD-ROM contains examples of displaying data.

This chapter also contains a section on working with tables. When you want to present text or numbers neatly in rows and columns, then it is worth using a table. PowerPoint uses **Microsoft® Word** to create tables so, if you are familiar with Word, you will have a head start.

Organisational charts

Learning objectives

● Create an organisational chart

● Amend an organisational chart

1.1 Creating an organisational chart

Exercise 1

Create an organisational chart on a slide as detailed below.

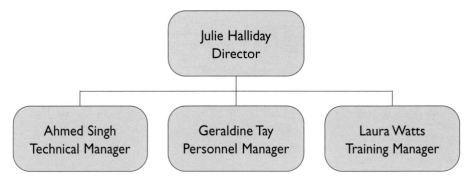

Creating an organisational chart
Double-click on chart placeholder of **AutoLayout**.

METHOD

1   Load PowerPoint and a new presentation.
2   Select: **Organization Chart AutoLayout** (see Figure 6.1).
3   Click on: **OK**.

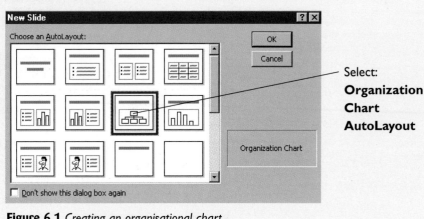

Select: **Organization Chart AutoLayout**

Figure 6.1 *Creating an organisational chart*

4   Change to **Slide View**.
5   Key in the title **Personnel** in the **Title** placeholder.
6   Double-click in the chart box to add the organisational chart. The **Organization Chart** window appears (see Figure 6.2). This contains a sample chart.
    Note: If you do not have Organization Chart installed, follow the instructions on screen to install it from the Office 2000 CD-ROM when prompted.
7   Overwrite **Chart Title** with the title: **Cybercafe Company**. Key in the details of personnel by clicking in the first relevant box and overwriting the original text. (Press: **Enter** to move to the following line.) Click on the second relevant box and so on. Press: **Esc** to finish.

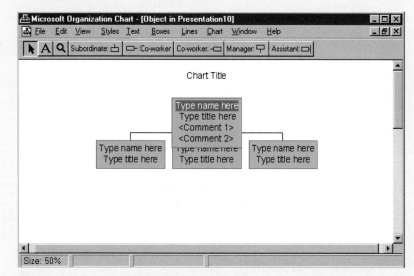

Figure 6.2 *Organization Chart* window containing sample chart

Adding chart boxes

Exercise 2

Simeon Hardie works alongside Ahmed Singh and is also a Technical Manager. Add a Co-worker box and enter his name and his position.

METHOD

1   Click on: the **Left Co-worker** button.
2   Click on Ahmed Singh's chart box and key in Simeon Hardie's details.

Exercise 3

Pat Hodge's line manager is Geraldine Tay. Her title is Administrator. Enter a chart box for Pat.

If you want to add
multiple boxes – e.g.
three co-worker
boxes – click three
times on: the **Co-
worker** button. This
works for all except
Manager. You can
continue adding as
many boxes as
necessary to complete
an organisational chart.

METHOD

1   Click on: the **Subordinate** button.
2   Click on Geraldine Tay's chart box and key in Pat Hodge's details.

To return to the slide, from the **File** menu in the **Chart** window, select
Exit and Return to [Presentation name] (see Figure 6.3).

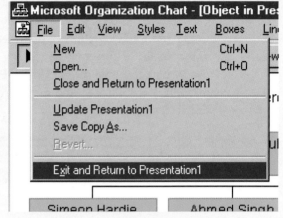

Figure 6.3 *Returning to the slide*

Information

**Inserting an organisational chart into a slide other
than the *Organizational Chart AutoLayout* that we
have chosen for this exercise**

1   From the **Insert** menu, select: **Object**.
2   The **Insert Object** dialogue box is displayed.
3   Ensure the **Create new** option button is chosen.
4   Select: **MS Organization Chart 2.0**.

1.2   Amending an organisational chart

You may want to update the organisational chart – for example, when
employees start, leave or change posts. You will also want to format the
chart to fit in with the presentation formatting and colour scheme.

Exercise 4

Access the organisational chart created in **Section 1.1**.

METHOD

1   Double-click on the chart.
2   The **Organization Chart** window is displayed.

Exercise 5

Make the following changes to the chart:
Pat Hodge is now Senior Administrator and she has an assistant
James Bond whose title is Administrator.
Ahmed Singh has left the company. Delete his details.

METHOD

1   Click on the box for Pat Hodge and key in her new title.
2   Click on the **Assistant** button, then on Pat Hodge's box.
3   Key in the new name and title.

Deleting a box

4   Select Ahmed Singh's box and press: **Delete**.

Exercise 6

Change the style of the chart.

METHOD

1   Select the entire chart by pressing **Ctrl + A**.
2   From the **Styles** menu, select the style you require.

Exercise 7

Change the font to **Times New Roman, 14 pt**. Change the text box fill
colour to **light grey** and the font to **red**.

METHOD

1   Select the entire chart (**Ctrl + A**).
2   Right-click on the chart and select from the pop-up menu or use
    the drop-down menus to reformat as requested.

Information

Selecting within the chart

Select parts of the chart by clicking on them while holding down the **Shift** key.

Moving boxes

METHOD

Use drag and drop (this will take subordinates).
Use **Edit** menu, **Cut** and **Paste** to move individuals only.

Other organisational chart options

Examine and practise other options available to individualise your chart using the drop-down and pop-up menus – for example, enlarging the chart, enlarging boxes.

Resizing the chart

METHOD

Select the chart and resize it using its handles.

Learning objectives

- Insert a data chart
- Types of chart
- Format a chart
- About a datasheet
- Insert an Excel chart

2.1 Inserting a data chart

Exercise 1

Create a slide containing the title: **Weekly Sales – January to March 2000**. Include a comparative column chart showing the sales set out below:

	Week 1	Week 2	Week 3	Week 4
Jan	106	98	270	106
Feb	49	50	98	200
Mar	208	41	111	119

Hint

There are three **AutoLayouts** containing charts. If you want to insert a chart into a slide that does not contain a chart placeholder, from the **Insert** menu, select: **Chart**.

METHOD

1 Open a new presentation.
2 Select **Chart AutoLayout** (see Figure 6.4).
3 Click on: **OK**.
4 Change to **Slide View**.

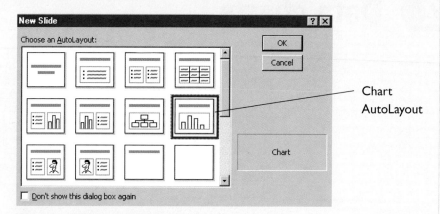

Figure 6.4 *Chart AutoLayout*

5   Key in the title in the **Title** placeholder.
6   Double-click in the **Chart** placeholder to add the chart. A datasheet containing sample data, a chart (see Figure 6.5) and charting menus and toolbar buttons appear (see Figure 6.6).
Note: If you do not have Graph installed, follow the instructions on screen to install it from the Office 2000 CD-ROM when prompted.

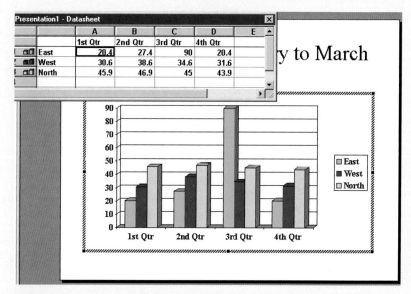

Figure 6.5 *Datasheet and chart*

Figure 6.6 *Charting menu and toolbar button options*

7   Key in the data as above (Exercise 1) in the appropriate cells, overwriting the sample data using the arrow keys to move from cell to cell.

8 Click on the **View Datasheet** button (see Figure 6.6) to display the chart only (see Figure 6.7).

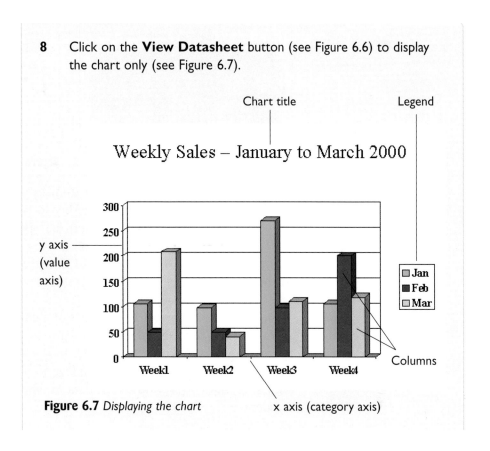

Figure 6.7 *Displaying the chart*

2.2 Types of chart

The most commonly used charts include column/bar charts, line graphs, comparative charts and pie charts.

Note: In the UK, we usually tend to differentiate between charts and graphs. For our purposes we can assume that they are the same thing.

A column chart (see Figure 6.8) uses columns to represent values. The chart has two axes, the *x* (horizontal axis) and the *y* (vertical axis). The *x* axis usually represents data that does not change, such as days of the week. The *y* axis usually represents values that fluctuate, such as monetary values or temperatures. This type of chart is useful for showing comparisons.

A bar chart (see Figure 6.9) has the same components as the column chart but shows the categories vertically and the values horizontally.

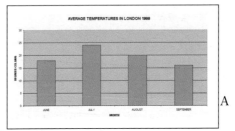

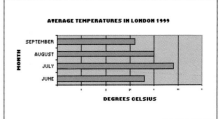

A

Figure 6.8 *Column chart*   **Figure 6.9** *Bar chart*

line graph (see Figure 6.10) shows trends in data at equal intervals. Points on the graph are joined together to form a continuous line. It has properties in common with a column/bar graph.

A **comparative chart** (see Figure 6.11) is used to compare sets of data as in the exercise above.

A **pie chart** (see Figure 6.12) consists of a circle divided into a number of segments that represent data. Each segment can have a value or percentage (of the whole data) label. In the example shown 30% of tutor group A have green eyes. There is a legend to show the colour/shaded segments that correspond to the data or labels can be added to each segment.

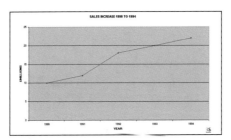

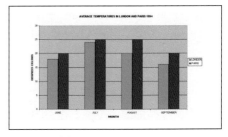

Figure 6.10 *Line graph*   **Figure 6.11** *Comparative chart*

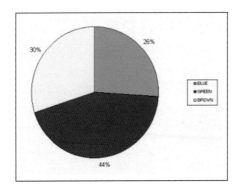

Figure 6.12 *Pie chart*

Parts of a chart

Chart Title	This should be descriptive and clear.
Bars/Segments	These represent the different values.
Legend	Key showing the different colours/shades that correspond to the data represented in the chart.

Exercise 2

Change the column chart to a 3-D bar chart.

Hint

Depending on how you lay out the data you can use the toolbar buttons to plot by row or by column. You can also create other types of chart – e.g. pie charts.

METHOD

1   Double-click on the chart to select it.
2   Click on: the **Chart Type** button arrow and select: **3-D Bar Chart**.
3   The chart changes into the requested chart.

2.3   Formatting a chart

Accessing options for formatting a chart

METHOD

1   Double-click on the chart to select it.
2   Right-click on an element of the chart and select from a pop-up menu as shown in Figures 6.13, 6.14 and 6.15.

(See the PowerPoint file **Numerical data** on the CD-ROM for examples of charts. Consult PowerPoint's online help if you need more detail.)

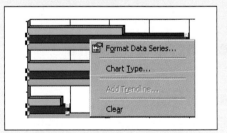

Figure 6.13 *Bars/columns* menu

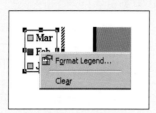

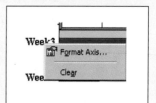

Figure 6.14 *Legend* menu   **Figure 6.15** *Axis* menu

2.4 More about the datasheet

If you are not familiar with the Excel spreadsheet application, you may find it useful to examine the datasheet more carefully. Different parts of the datasheet are labelled in Figure 6.16.

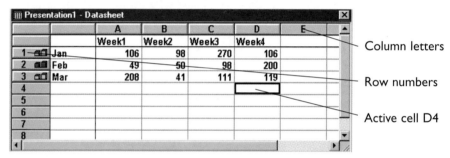

Figure 6.16 *Parts of a datasheet*

Moving around the datasheet

METHOD

Use the arrow keys or click on the cell you want to become active.

Selecting a cell range

METHOD

Click on the first cell and drag the mouse over the other cells in the range.

Selecting the entire datasheet

METHOD

Press: **Ctrl +A**.

Deleting cell contents

METHOD

Select the cell(s) containing the contents to be deleted. Press: **Delete**.

Inserting rows

METHOD

1   Select the row by clicking in the **row ref** box (at the side of the row) below the one where you want the new row to appear.
2   Right-click. From the pop-up menu, select: **Insert**.

Inserting columns

METHOD

1   Select the column by clicking in the **column ref** box (at the top of the column) following the one where you want the new column to appear.
2   Right-click. From the pop-up menu, select: **Insert**.

Deleting rows

METHOD

1   Select the row by clicking in the **row ref** box (at the side of the row) that you want to delete.
2   Right-click. From the pop-up menu, select: **Delete**.

Deleting columns

METHOD

1 Select the column by clicking in the **column ref** box (at the top of the column) that you want to delete.
2 Right-click. From the pop-up menu, select: **Delete**.

Changing column width

METHOD

Using the mouse, drag the column border (see Figure 6.17) *or* double-click on the column border to exactly fit the contents into the cell.

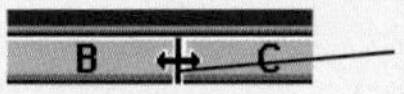

Column border

Figure 6.17 *Changing column width*

2.5 Inserting an Excel chart

METHOD

1 Display the slide on which you want the chart to appear in **Slide View**.
2 Open Excel and the file containing the chart.
3 Select the chart and click on Excel's **Copy** button. The chart will be pasted to the clipboard (you will not see or be advised of this).
4 Close Excel.
5 Click on PowerPoint's **Paste** button.
6 The chart is placed on the slide.
7 Resize and position it as necessary.
8 Format the chart using the same methods as for those created within PowerPoint.

Learning objectives

● Insert a table   ● Adjust a table

3.1 Inserting a table into a slide

Exercise 1

Using the table facility, produce a slide in a new presentation displaying the following:

Wind speed – Beaufort scale

Number	Description	Characteristics
0	Calm	Smoke goes straight up
3	Gentle breeze	Extends a light flag
6	Strong breeze	Umbrellas hard to use

Hint

If you have not used the **Table AutoLayout**, from the **Insert** menu, select: **Table**.

METHOD

1   Load PowerPoint and a new presentation.
2   Select: **Table AutoLayout** (see Figure 6.18).

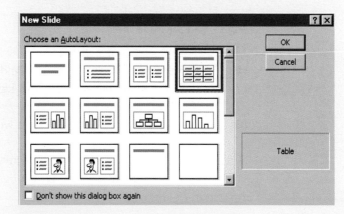

Figure 6.18 *Selecting Table AutoLayout*

3 Change to **Slide View**.

4 Key in the title in the **Title** placeholder.

5 Double-click in the **Table** placeholder.

6 The **Insert Table** dialogue box is displayed (see Figure 6.19).

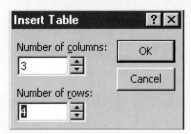

Figure 6.19 *Selecting numbers of rows and columns*

7 Select the numbers of columns and rows (columns go down, rows go across) using the up/down arrows, in this case, 3 columns and 4 rows (maximum is 25 by 25).

8 Click on: **OK**.

9 The slide is displayed with an empty table inserted (see Figure 6.20). Each box is called a cell. The **Tables and Borders** toolbar also appears.

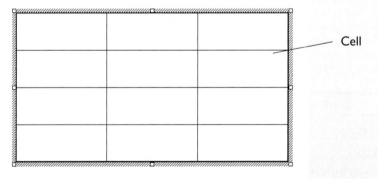

Figure 6.20 *Slide with table*

10 Click in the top left cell to select it and key in: **Number**.

11 Move to the next cell using the **Tab** key.

12 Key in: **Description**.

13 Repeat steps **10** to **12** to fill all cells with the appropriate text.

Note: Do not press **Tab** after the final entry as this will create another row. If you have done this, use the **Undo** button. The table will look like the one in Figure 6.21.

Wind speed – Beaufort scale

Number	Description	Characteristics
0	Calm	Smoke goes straight up
3	Gentle breeze	Extends a light flag
6	Strong breeze	Umbrellas hard to use

Figure 6.21 *Text entered into table*

3.2 Adjusting a table

The table can now be adjusted to suit. Use the following as a guide.

Changing column width/row height

METHOD

Either

1   Position the cursor on the column/row border. The pointer becomes a double-headed arrow (see Figure 6.22).
2   Drag to the required position.

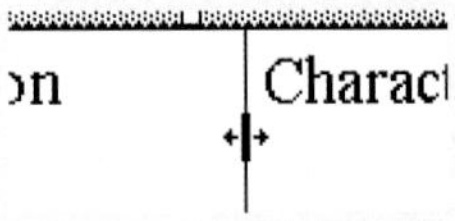

)n | Charac

Figure 6.22 *Adjusting column width*

> *or*
> Double-click on the column/row border so that the contents of the cell fit exactly.

Selecting cells

METHOD

Drag across the cells.

Selecting a table

Formatting table properties

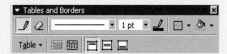

Figure 6.23 *Tables and Borders toolbar*

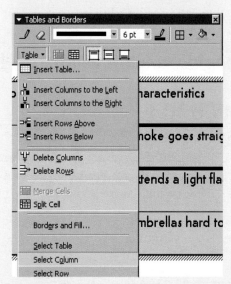

Figure 6.24 *Clicking on the down-arrow of the Table button displays more choices*

Practise your skills

1   Open a new PowerPoint presentation, choose a suitable design template to be used throughout and create the following four slides:

Slide 1
Using the **Title Slide** layout enter the title: **Arts Department, North Weston College** and the sub-title: **Friarsmith Mansion, Heathcliff Road, Leeds LS6 9YQ e-mail arts@nwc.ac.uk**.

Slide 2
Using the **Organization Chart** layout, enter the title: **Structure of Arts**. Enter the organisational chart below with the title: **Current Staff**:

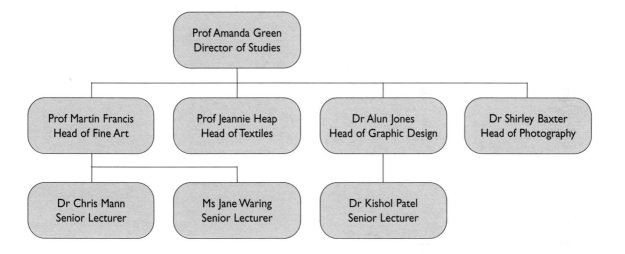

Slide 3
Using the **Chart slide** layout, add the title: **Number of Students**. Use the following chart data to produce a 3-D bar chart.

	Art	Text	Graphics	Photo
TERM 1	28	36	20	18
TERM 2	61	43	39	50
TERM 3	25	41	60	70

Slide 4

Using the **Table** slide layout, create the following table. Use the title: **Room Allocation**.

	Art	Textiles	Photography
Monday	Studio 6	Lecture Hall	Admin Room
Wednesday	Studio 1	Textiles 1	Lecture Hall
Thursday	Studio 6	Admin Room	Outdoors
Saturday	Lecture Hall	Textiles 1	Indoors

2   Save the presentation and print the slides on separate pages.
3   Close the presentation.

Chapter 7 Creating a slide show

Introduction

This chapter gives instructions for viewing your slides as a slide show on a computer screen or using a computer attached to a projection device. There are many options available to set up and view the show. If you are going to be a live speaker at the show, then you may want to run the show manually or automate it so that a slide disappears and the next one appears with a timing delay that you have set. You may want to set up an unattended, self-running presentation that can loop so that it is played over and over.

Whatever you decide you will be able to add special effects to make the presentation more interesting and enjoyable. Beware of too much excitement – limit the effects!

The CD-ROM contains the PowerPoint file **Effects** that demonstrates a variety of special slide-show effects.

This chapter also contains instructions for adding links from one place to another in the form of **Action Buttons** and hyperlinks. These make the presentation interactive. Note: If you are hyperlinking to a page on the Internet it could take some time to download, so be prepared.

Note: You can also set up a show for an online meeting or for presenting over the Internet. These options are covered in the **Appendix**.

1 **Automating a presentation**

Learning objectives

- View slides in a slide show
- Create transitional timings
- Start a slide show
- Change transitional timings
- Create transitional effects
- Create preset animation effects
- Hide slides

- Reorder slides
- Delete slides
- Write on slides
- Shortcut keys during a slide show
- Add sound
- Run a slide show from a laptop or projection system

1.1 **Viewing slides in Slide Show View**

Exercise 1

Note: For this exercise you will need to access the CD-ROM and load the PowerPoint file: **Slide Shows**.

View the presentation by advancing slides manually.

METHOD

1. Load PowerPoint and the presentation file: **Slide Shows**.
2. Ensure that the presentation is set at slide 1.
3. Change to **Slide Show View**.
4. Use the **Page Down** key or click the mouse to advance to the next slide until you have viewed the five slides in the presentation.

Information

Slide Show View

In **Slide Show View** you can see how the slides look on a full screen. Use **Page Up/Page Down** to move to the next/previous slide (other keys perform the same task as in other views – use **Home** to go to Slide 1 and use **End** to go to the last slide). Pressing: **Esc** returns you to the original view.

1.2 Creating transitional timings

The slides do not advance automatically until transitional timings (slide durations) options are set. You can set these as required so that a slide is shown for a set amount of time before advancing automatically to the next slide.

Exercise 2

Automate the presentation with slide durations as shown below:

SLIDE NO	SLIDE DURATION
Slide 1	5 sec
Slide 2	7 sec
Slide 3	15 sec
Slide 4	10 sec
Slide 5	10 sec

Handy reference

Slide transitions
Slide Sorter View,
Slide Transition
button.

METHOD

1   Change to **Slide Sorter View**, click on Slide 1 to select it.
2   Click on the 🗗 **Slide Transition** button.
3   The **Slide Transition** dialogue box appears (see Figure 7.1).

Figure 7.1 *Slide Transition dialogue box*

4   In the **Advance** section, click in the box **On mouse click** so that there is no tick in the box. Click in the box **Automatically after** so that a tick is shown, and in the box beneath, key in the slide duration (or use the up button) for Slide 1 (i.e. 5) (see Figure 7.2).

Figure 7.2 *Selecting timing*

5   Click on **Apply**. Slide 1 now has the duration (05) shown underneath at the left-hand side (see Figure 7.3).

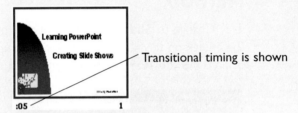

Figure 7.3 *Transitional timing*

6   Repeat steps 2 to 5 for each of the other slides, ensuring you have selected the timing requested for this exercise.

7   Save the presentation with a new name.

Figure 7.4 *Rehearsal box*

1.3 Starting a slide show

Handy reference

Starting a slide show
Slide Show menu,
View Show.

Exercise 3

Start the slide show created in **Section 1.2**.

METHOD

1   From the **Slide Show** menu, select: **View Show**.
2   The presentation will run automatically with the timings that have been set.

1.4 Changing transitional timings

If you are not happy with the timings set, change them by selecting a slide, in **Slide Sorter View**, with the time you want to change.

Hint

If you right-click the mouse while the presentation is running, you can select other useful options – e.g. **Pause** the presentation or **Blank Screen**.

METHOD

1   Click on: the **Slide Transition** button.
2   Edit the time next to the **Automatically** after box.
3   Click on: **Apply**.
4   Repeat for any other slides you want to change.

1.5 Creating transitional effects

These effects control how slides appear on the screen during transitions. They are used to enhance the display and so help maintain audience concentration.

Exercise 4

Create different transition effects for each of the slides

Handy reference

Transitional effects
Slide Sorter View,
**Slide Transition
Effects** button.

METHOD

1   Click on: the **Slide Sorter View** button.
2   Click on Slide 1 to select it.
3   Click on the down arrow on the **Slide Transition Effects** box (see Figure 7.5).

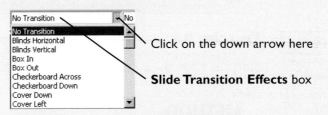

Click on the down arrow here

Slide Transition Effects box

Figure 7.5 *Creating **Slide Transition Effects***

4   A drop-down menu appears. There are many transition effects to choose from – you can scroll down for more. Click on a transition effect – you will instantly see a preview of the effect on Slide 1. Experiment with the different effects. When you find one you like, leave it visible in the **Slide Transition Effects** box.

5   An icon appears beneath the slide to show that it has a transition effect applied to it (see Figure 7.6).

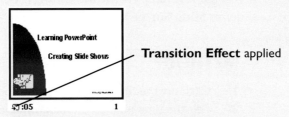

Transition Effect applied

Figure 7.6 *Applying a **Transition Effect***

6   Repeat for the other slides, choosing a different transitional effect for each one.

7   Save the presentation.

8   You can now run the presentation so that you can see how the transitional effects look.

Hint

To delete a **transition effect**, select the slide. Click on: **No Transition** on the **Slide Transition Effects** drop-down list.

Information

Applying a transition effect to more than one slide

If you want to apply the same transition effect to more than one slide in the presentation, select more than one slide by holding down **Ctrl** while clicking on them. It is best not to apply too many transition effects to an automated presentation. You can refine the transition effect further by clicking on: the **Slide Transition** button so that the **Slide Transition** dialogue box appears. Here you can choose the speed of the effect and add sound!

Preset animation effects determine the way that text and other objects are revealed on a slide. They are particularly effective when applied to bulleted lists but can be applied to any slide object to give text and other objects more of an impact.

Exercise 5

Experiment by adding different preset animation (build) effects to the bulleted slide 4.

Handy reference

Preset animation effects
Slide Sorter View,
Preset Animation box.

Hint

You may need to change to **Slide View**, select the text on the appropriate slide using the **Edit** menu, **Select All**. Then from the **Slide Show** menu, select: **Preset Animation**.

METHOD

1   Click on: the **Slide Sorter View** button.
2   Click on Slide 4 to select it.
3   Click on the down arrow on the **Preset Animation** toolbar box (see Figure 7.7).

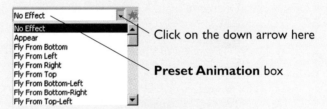

Click on the down arrow here

Preset Animation box

Figure 7.7 *Setting a **Build Effect***

4   A drop-down menu appears. There are many effects to choose from – you can scroll down for more. Click on an effect.
5   An icon appears beneath the slide to show that an animation effect has been applied to it (see Figure 7.8).

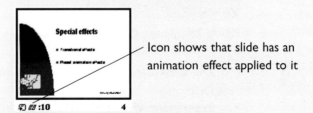

Icon shows that slide has an animation effect applied to it

Figure 7.8 *Preset animation effect applied*

6   To view the animation effect, change to **Slide Show View**. The presentation will begin. To exit the slide show, press: **Esc**.
7   Try other preset animation effects.
8   Save the presentation.
9   View the automated presentation.

Deleting a preset animation effect

METHOD

1   Select the slide.
2   From the **Preset Animation** box drop-down menu, select: **No effect**.

Creating custom effects

METHOD

1   You can create custom effects by right-clicking on the element you want to animate in **Slide View**.
2   Select: **Custom Animation** from the pop-up menu (see Figure 7.9).

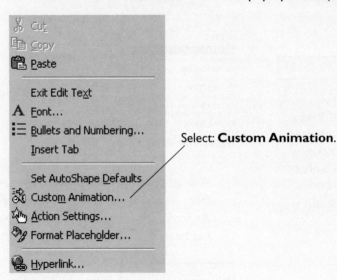

Select: **Custom Animation**.

Figure 7.9 *Creating* ***Custom Animation***

3   The **Custom Animation** dialogue box is displayed (see Figure 7.10).
4   Experiment with the different options.
5   Select different objects (e.g. text to add various effects – such as spiral, zoom – or charts to practise building them up bar by bar).

Hint

The **Custom Animation** dialogue box is very useful when you are fine-tuning slides. It is also useful to access it when viewing presentations that have been prepared by someone else, in order to find out what effects they have applied.

6 Set timings and other properties by clicking on the relevant tabs and making selections.

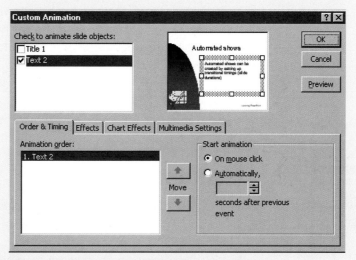

Figure 7.10 *Custom Animation dialogue box*

Information

Starting at a slide other than 1

To start the slide show at a slide other than the first slide, select: **Set Up Show** from the **Slide Show** menu. The **Set Up Show** dialogue box is displayed (see Figure 7.11). In the **Slides** section, key in the slides to view. Note the other options available in this dialogue box that you might find useful.

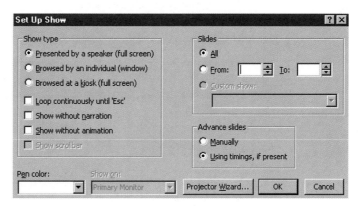

Figure 7.11 *Set Up Show dialogue box*

1.7 Hiding slides

You may have a slide in your presentation that you want to keep in the presentation but do not want to show in the slide show – for example, the information it contains might be confidential or it might contain prices that have not been updated. In such a case, you can choose to hide the slide.

Exercise 6

Hide one of the slides in your show.

Handy reference

Hiding Slides
Slide Sorter View,
Hide Slide button.

METHOD

1   In **Slide Sorter View**, select the slide to hide.
2   Click on: the 🔲 **Hide Slide** button.

Hidden slides have a cross through their number: 🔲

1.8 Reordering slides

You may decide to change the slide order in a presentation.

METHOD

1   Change to **Slide Sorter View**.
2   Hold down the left mouse button on the slide to move and drag it to the required position.

1.9 Deleting slides

METHOD

1   In **Slide Sorter View**, select the slide to delete by clicking on it.
2   Press: **Delete**.

Note: Instructions for reordering and deleting slides have already been given but are repeated here in case you need reminding.

1.10 Writing on slides

Sometimes it is useful to be able to circle certain words or make a note on a slide during a presentation. However, use this sparingly as it can look messy because mouse control can be difficult, especially if you are nervous.

METHOD

I	Set up the pen colour from the **Slide Show** menu by selecting: **Set Up Show**.
2	With the slide show running, wait until the slide you want to write on has finished loading.
3	Press: **Ctrl + P** to access the pen.
4	Drag the mouse to draw or write on the slide.
5	To delete the drawing, press: **E**.
6	To delete the drawing and move to the next slide, press: **N**.

1.11 During a slide show

The following table shows shortcut keys that can be used to perform various actions during a full-screen show.

Action	Keys
Go to next slide	**N, Enter, Page Down**, right arrow (→), down arrow (↓), spacebar (or click mouse)
Go to previous slide	**P, Page up**, left arrow (←), up arrow (↑), backspace
Go to a particular slide	[Slide no] + **Enter**
Display a black screen	**B**
Display a white screen	**W**
Stop or restart a slide show	**S** or plus sign (+)
End a slide show	**Esc**
See list of controls during a slide show	**F1**
Hide pointer	**Ctrl + H**
Redisplay pointer	**Ctrl + P**

1.12 Adding sound to objects in a slide show

You can add sound to objects so that, when you hover the mouse over the object, the sound plays.

Exercise 7

Insert a graphic image on the final slide of the presentation. Add a suitable sound that will play when the mouse hovers over the graphic image.

METHOD

1   In **Slide View**, display the final slide.
2   Insert a suitable graphic image.
3   Right-click on the image and select: **Action Settings** from the pop-up menu.
4   The **Action Settings** dialogue box is displayed (see Figure 7.12).

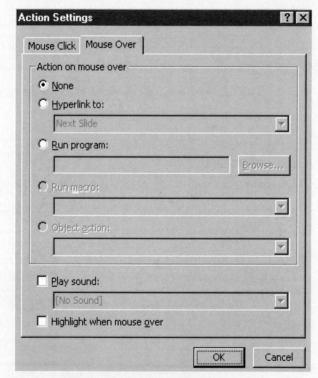

Figure 7.12 *Inserting a sound on mouse over*

5   Select: the **Mouse Over** tab.
6   Click in the **Play Sound** box so that a tick appears and select a suitable sound.
7   Run the presentation to hear the effect.

1.13 Running a slide show from a laptop computer and a projection system

METHOD

1   Connect your laptop computer to the projection system (consult your laptop documentation).
2   From the **Slide Show** menu, select: **Set Up Show**.
3   The **Set Up Show** dialogue box is displayed.
4   Click on the **Projector Wizard** button.
5   Follow the wizard's instructions.

Note: Some common problems associated with setting up projected slide shows are addressed in the **Appendix**.

2 Adding Action Buttons and hyperlinks

Learning objectives

- About **Action Buttons** and hyperlinks
- **Action Buttons** in action
- Add **Action Buttons** and **Action Settings**
- Create hyperlinks

2.1 What are Action Buttons and hyperlinks?

Action Buttons and hyperlinks can be added to a presentation to make it interactive. When you click on an **Action Button** it can be set up to perform some action – for example, jump to another slide with relevant information, provide help, access a website or a shortcut to run another program. A hyperlink performs the same type of action but can be attached to any selected object on a slide and does not need to be assigned to an **Action Button**. When you click on the hyperlink object you will be taken to a pre-determined destination. An **Action Button** can have a defined hyperlink so that it too jumps to its pre-determined destination when clicked.

2.2 Action Buttons in action

Open the PowerPoint presentation file **Hotel** on the CD-ROM. This is a six-slide presentation about Hotel Accommodation. The first slide is the title slide. Slide 2 (see Figure 7.13) contains two **Action Buttons**. View the show (ensuring slide 1 is selected) by changing to **Slide Show View**. When you click on the **2 star hotel Action Button**, the relevant slide about 2 Star hotels is displayed and a sound is played. The **2 star hotel** slide (see Figure 7.14) also contains an **Action Button** to take you back to where you started from. These **Action Buttons** have pre-defined hyperlinks that link to the relevant slides. Now try the **3 star hotel Action Button** and return to slide 2.

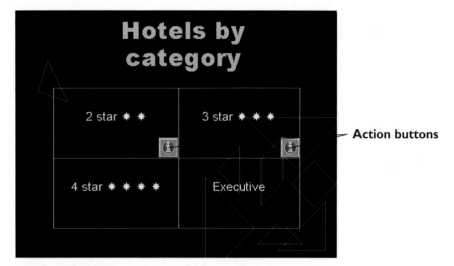

Figure 7.13 *Slide 2*

Figure 7.14 *Slide containing information on 2 star hotels*

2.3 Adding Action Buttons and Action Settings

Exercise 1

Add an **Action Button** and **Action Settings** to Slide 2 for the 4 star hotels that links to the relevant slide. Add an **Action Button** and **Action Settings** to the 4 star hotels slide that returns to Slide 2.

Handy reference
Adding *Action* buttons Slide Show menu, **Action Buttons**.

METHOD

1 Display Slide 2 in **Slide View**.
2 From the **Slide Show** menu, select: **Action Buttons** and click on the relevant icon (see Figure 7.15).

Figure 7.15 *Adding Action Buttons*

Hint

Copying *Action* **Buttons**
You can copy **Action Buttons** by right-clicking on them and selecting: **Paste**. They copy their attributes with them so you will need to redefine these.

3   A cross hair appears on the slide.
4   Click the left mouse **button**.
5   The **Action Settings** dialogue box is displayed (see Figure 7.16).

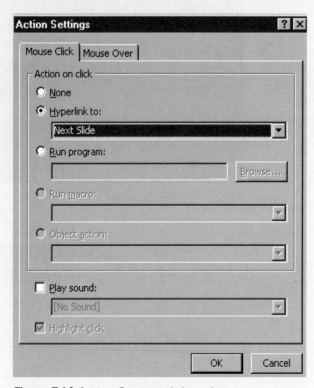

Figure 7.16 *Action Settings* dialogue box

6   With the **Mouse Click** tab selected (notice you can select **Mouse Over** too), in the **Action on click** section, click in the **Hyperlink to** option button.
7   Click on the down arrow and on **Slide ...** (see Figure 7.17).

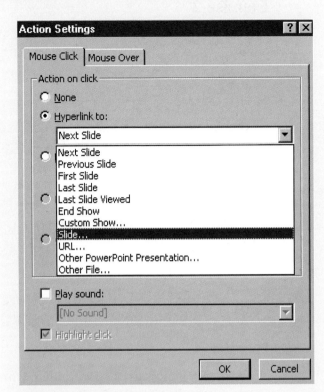

Figure 7.17 *Hyperlink possibilities*

8   The **Hyperlink to Slide** dialogue box is displayed (see Figure 7.18).

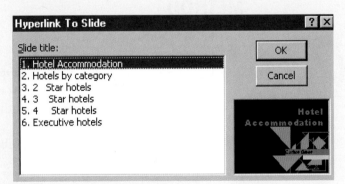

Figure 7.18 *Hyperlink to Slide box*

9   Click on: slide **5, 4 Star Hotels** to select it.
10   Click on: **OK**.
11   Click in the **Play Sound** box and add a **Drive By** sound from the drop-down menu.
12   Click on: **OK**.
13   Size and position the **Action Button** as appropriate.
14   Run the slide show to see the effect.

Hint

Action Button sounds are optional.

Exercise 2

Add an **Action Button** (as on slides 3 and 4) to Slide 5 that returns to Slide 2.

> **METHOD**
>
> Use the method above, but choose a different style **Action Button**. Hyperlink to Slide 2 and use the **Camera** sound effect.

Exercise 3

Repeat the process so that Executive Hotels are linked to the relevant slide and back again. Run the slide show again to see the effects.

2.4 Creating hyperlinks

Exercise 4

Note: This exercise uses the Word file **Carlton Green** on the CD-ROM. Create a hyperlink for the **Carlton Green** text on slide 1 that takes you to the Word file **Carlton Green**. This file contains information about Carlton Green.

> **METHOD**
>
> 1 In **Slide View**, with Slide 1 displayed, select the text **Carlton Green**.
> 2 Right-click on the text and select: **Hyperlink**.
> 3 The **Edit Hyperlink** dialogue box is displayed (see Figure 7.19).
> 4 In the **Browse for** section click on: the **File** button to locate the file. Locate the file and click on: **OK**. Its full location is automatically entered in the **Type the file or Web page name** box. (In this example I have copied the file to my C drive in **My documents** folder.)
> 5 Click on: **OK**.
> 6 Run the slide show and use the hyperlink to access the **Carlton Green** file to check that it functions correctly.
> 7 Close **Word**.
> 8 You are returned to the presentation.
> 9 Save the presentation.

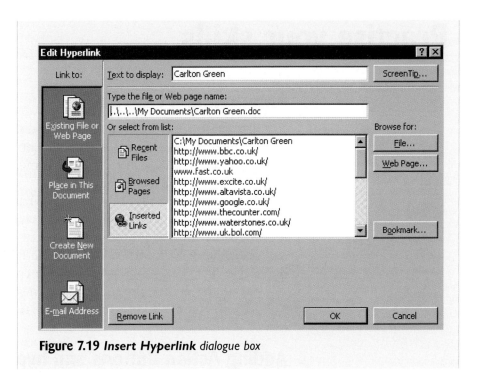

Figure 7.19 *Insert Hyperlink dialogue box*

Note: For more information on **Action Buttons** and hyperlinks, PowerPoint's online help is very informative.

Practise your skills

Automating a slide show

1   Open a suitable presentation that you have created or that is available on the CD-ROM which is not already automated.
2   Automate the slide show. Include some special effects that you have discovered in this chapter.
3   View the show and make notes on what you like and do not like about different effects. Ask yourself why?
4   View the show again this time concentrating on what would work and what would not work with an audience you might have.
5   Revise the effects so that the automated slide show flows freely and the effects do not distract from the message.
6   Save the presentation with a new file name.

Adding Action Buttons and hyperlinks

1   Create the following PowerPoint presentation using any design of your choice.

Slide number	Content
1	**Language Learning Company** www.llcx.edu.uk
2	**Languages** French German Spanish
3	French Courses
4	German Course
5	Spanish Courses

2   On slide 1 add a hyperlink to the website address (**Note:** It is a fictitious address. If you prefer you could use a proper address to check that it works.)
3   On slide 2, add **Action** buttons with defined hyperlinks that access the relevant French, German and Spanish pages.
4   On slides 3, 4 and 5, add **Action** buttons to return to Slide 2.
5   Save the presentation.

Chapter 8 Using a scanner, digital camera, video camera or sound to individualise your presentation

Introduction

There are times when using only your own customised creations will do to deliver the message effectively. For instance, you may want to add the company logo from the headed paper, that special photo of the team at work or a narration by a leading expert. If you have access to a scanner, a digital camera or video camera then you will be able to import your own pictures and video clips into PowerPoint. You can also capture or create sound to incorporate into the presentation. Remember to adhere to copyright conditions for any pre-recorded material.

Multimedia production is a vast topic and merits a book all of its own. This chapter is only able to cover a bare minimum for you to get started so that you can decide whether or not to delve further. Be warned it is quite addictive!

Multimedia files can be very large so you will need to ensure that your computer meets the requirements to cope with graphics and sound effectively. If not it will be a very slow and tedious presentation, both in the production and delivery stages. Use the following as a guide:

- A minimum of 32 MB RAM, preferably 64 MB or more
- A high capacity hard disk drive with free space, minimum capacity 2 GB, preferably 8 GB

- A fast microprocessor, preferably 500 MHz or more
- If you plan to record your own sound, you will need an audio input on your computer and a microphone.

Checking the RAM on your computer

1 Right-click on: **My Computer** icon.
2 Select: **Properties** from the pop-up menu.
3 The **System Properties** window is displayed.
4 Here you will see the amount of RAM listed.
5 Click on: **OK**.

Checking hard drive disk space

1 Double-click on: **My Computer** icon.
2 **My Computer** window is displayed.
3 Right-click on: **Drive C** icon.
4 Select: **Properties** from the pop-up menu.
5 The **Local disk (C:) Properties** dialogue box is displayed.
6 Here the hard drive's **Free space** is listed.
7 Click on: **OK**.

Checking the microprocessor speed

This is not easy. Check your computer receipt and you may see the microprocessor speed listed there. Otherwise some PCs display this information when they are first switched on, but don't blink or you will miss it!

Note: There are multimedia examples in the PowerPoint file **Milton Keynes** on the CD-ROM.

1 Using a scanner or digital camera

Learning objectives

- Import from a scanner or digital camera
- Use a video camera

- Change screen settings
- Adjust graphic or video clip for screen resolution

1.1 Importing directly from a scanner or digital camera

Handy reference

Importing from scanner or digital camera
Insert menu, **Picture**, **From Scanner or Camera**.

METHOD

1. Ensure the scanner or digital camera is connected to the computer (consult user manuals).
2. Load PowerPoint and the presentation.
3. Display the slide in **Slide View** where you want the image to be placed.
4. From the **Insert** menu, select: **Picture, From Scanner or Camera**.
5. The **Insert Picture from Scanner or Camera** dialogue box is displayed (see Figure 8.1).

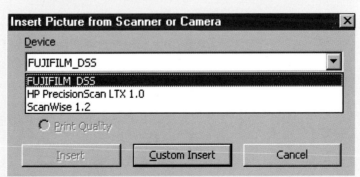

Figure 8.1 *Inserting a picture*

6. Click on the down arrow of the **Device** box and select the device.
7. Click on: **Custom Insert**.
8. The scanner will scan the image or you will need to follow the instructions for your particular digital camera.
9. You are now able to edit your image using the **Picture** toolbar buttons (**View** menu, **Toolbars**, **Picture** and see **Chapter 5**, **Section 2**).

Information

File types

If you have image editing software – for example, Photo Editor, Photoshop, Photoshop Deluxe, Paint Shop Pro – you will be able to save a picture file in a number of formats. You will also be able to manipulate it in various ways with quite stunning results (see the photo files on the CD-ROM in the **Textures/Effects** folder for examples). Once you have finished editing you can then insert the final file into PowerPoint using the **Insert** menu, **Picture**, **From File**.

Using the **Insert** menu is preferable to using the *cut and paste* insertion method, because the resulting file size is usually smaller. PowerPoint can import many different file types (some need to use a special filter from the Office CD-ROM and you will be led through its installation if appropriate). It is worth experimenting to see which file types work best in your presentation. The following are probably the safest choices:

- **JPEG** format is good for photographic images because it uses millions of colours. It is a compressed image format which means that the file takes up less disk space.
- **GIF** images are good for line drawings or greyscales. Their limitation is that they use only 256 colours.
- **BMP** files are good at maintaining quality but are stored in an uncompressed format so take up a lot of storage space.
- **TIFF** files are also good quality but can be huge in size.

Try saving the same file in the different formats and then check the sizes using **File** menu, **Properties**, **General** tab.

1.2 Using a video camera

There are specialised companies that will create video clips or convert video footage that you already have into a format suitable for your use. If you have a video camera and your computer has a very high specification and a video capture card, you can create customised video files (this is beyond the scope of this book) that can be inserted into PowerPoint presentations. Although video files are usually compressed they still take up a lot of storage space. They are usually files of type AVI, MOV or MPG.

METHOD

1   Open PowerPoint and the presentation and slide where you want to add the video clip.
2   Change to **Slide View**.
3   From the **Insert** menu, select: **Movies and Sounds, Movie from File**.
4   Locate the file and click on: **Open**.
5   PowerPoint will ask if you want to play the movie automatically. Click on: **Yes** if you do. Click on: **No** if you want it to play when you click on it.

If showing your presentation on a PC, it may be better to use the AVI file format. This uses Windows Media Player (included with Windows) to display the video. Since video files do not become part of the presentation but instead are linked, it is best to ensure that the video file is stored in the same folder as the presentation when you originally insert it. This is where PowerPoint will look first.

When viewing images or video you may need to alter screen settings for a better result.

1.3 Changing screen settings

METHOD

1   Double-click on: **My Computer** icon.
2   The **My Computer** window is displayed.
3   Click on: **Control Panel**.
4   Click on: **Display**.
5   The **Display Properties** dialogue box is displayed.
6   With the **Settings** tab selected, change the **Colors and Screen** area settings.

METHOD

1   Check the screen resolution on the computer that you will use for the presentation.
2   From the **Format** menu, select: **Picture**.
3   With the **Size** tab selected, in the **Scale** section, click in the **Best Scale for Slide Show** box.
4   Select the actual resolution from the drop-down menu.
5   Click on: **OK**.

2 Sound

Learning objectives

- Add a soundtrack
- Add narration

Handy reference

Inserting a soundtrack
Insert menu, **Movies and Sounds**, **Play CD Audio Track**.

METHOD

1 Display the slide in **Slide View** that you want sound attached to.
2 From the **Insert** menu, select **Movies and Sounds**, **Play CD Audio Track**.
3 The **Movie and Sound Options** dialogue box is displayed (see Figure 8.2).

Figure 8.2 *Inserting a sound from a CD*

4 Select the options that will suit your presentation.
5 Click on: **OK**.
6 You will be asked if you want to play the CD automatically. Click on: **Yes** if you do or on: **No** to play on mouse click or mouse over.
7 The slide will now have a CD icon.
8 Load the CD and view the slide show to hear the sound.

Hiding the CD icon while not playing

METHOD

1   From the **Slide Show** menu, select: **Custom Animation**.
2   With the **Order and Timing** tab selected, select the CD object in the **Animation Order** box.
3   Click on: the **Multimedia Settings** tab
4   Click in the **Hide while not playing** box.

Playing the CD across more than one slide

METHOD

1   Click in the **Continue Slide Show** box and then in the **Stop Playing After** button.
2   Key in the slide number.
3   Click on: **OK**.
4   Change to **Slide Show View** to see and hear the effect.

Note: Don't forget to have the CD in the drive and remember to take it with you when you deliver the presentation!

2.2 Adding narration (recording voice-over) to slides

Handy reference

Recording
narration
Slide Show menu,
Record Narration.

METHOD

1   Ensure your microphone is plugged into the correct socket of your computer (consult your documentation).
2   From the **Slide Show** menu, select: **Record Narration**.
3   The **Record Narration** dialogue box is displayed (see Figure 8.3).

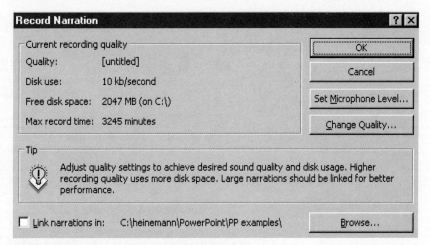

Figure 8.3 *Record Narration dialogue box*

4   Click on: the **Set Microphone Level** button.
5   The **Microphone Check** dialogue box is displayed (see Figure 8.4).
6   Follow the instructions in this box. (This only needs to be checked
     for the first recording.)

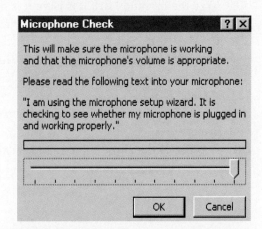

Figure 8.4 *Microphone Check dialogue box*

7   If the microphone is working the box above the slider will display
     coloured squares. (If it is not working check that it is plugged in
     properly to the correct socket.)
8   Click on: **OK**.
9   Click on: the **Change Quality** button.
10   The **Sound Selection** dialogue box is displayed (see Figure 8.5).

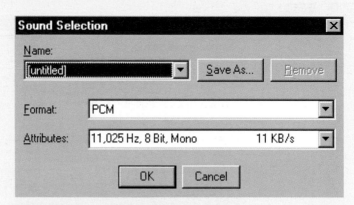

Figure 8.5 *Sound Selection* *dialogue box*

11 Select the quality from the **Attributes** drop-down list.
    Note: You will have to experiment with what works best, but do keep an eye on the presentation file size. Sound files can be very memory hungry.

12 Click on: **OK**.

13 Decide if you need to link the narration. (This will depend on how large the narration is. If it is large it is better to link it. This enables the file to be accessed when appropriate.)

14 Click on: **OK** again.

15 PowerPoint displays in **Slide Show View**.

16 Start narrating. Press: **Esc** when you have finished or continue until the end of the show.

17 You will be prompted to save with timings. Click on your preferences.

18 Run the **Slide Show** to see and hear the effect.

Information

Sound files

Sound files do not always become a part of the PowerPoint presentation. The presentation links to the sound file when it is run. If the file is linked, it is best to ensure that a sound file is stored in the same folder as the presentation file when preparing the presentation. Otherwise, if it has been inserted from elsewhere (especially if you are presenting on a computer other than that where you prepared the presentation), PowerPoint may not be able to locate it.

Practise your skills

There are many ways that you can practise the skills learnt in this chapter. Here are some ideas:

- Transfer a company logo from headed paper onto the master slide of a presentation.
- Transfer a company logo from a file onto the master slide of a presentation.
- Take a photo relevant to your presentation using a digital camera and insert it into your presentation.
- Find a relevant photo and scan it into your presentation.
- Add a soundtrack to a self-running presentation.
- Add narration to a slide show.
- Take some video footage and insert it into your presentation.

Note: Remember to address any copyright issues and be aware of file size.

Chapter 9 Preparing to deliver your presentation

Introduction

This chapter is divided into two sections. Section 1 addresses preparing your presentation for delivery. Section 2 concentrates on preparing yourself.

1 Preparing your presentation for delivery

Learning objectives

- Final checks
- Transfer the presentation
- Use **Pack and Go**
- Run the presentation

1.1 Making final checks

Check your slides thoroughly for any inconsistencies – for example, using open punctuation on one slide and not on another, capitalisation of main headings or not, font inconsistencies. You might find the **Style checker** useful here. Run the **spellchecker** again and check any words that you are unsure of in a dictionary. Remember the **spellchecker** may not always use the right word in the right context – for example, **We have no time to stand and stair** may look correct to the **spellchecker** but, in fact, it is using the wrong **stair** and should read **stare**. Print out and photocopy any notes and handouts ready for distribution.

Practise running through the entire show on the equipment that you will be using for the presentation (if possible) to see that the timings (if you have set any) and the slides are still relevant. No matter what timings you have set, the slides with more memory-hungry content, such as sound, graphics, will always take longer to load than simple text. Do not forget that a PowerPoint file does not store sound files and video files but has links to them so they will run when accessed. Check that you have these files and that they can be accessed. If you are running a CD soundtrack, remember to take it with you. Run through the show once before presenting. This helps to speed up any otherwise slow-loading content.

It cannot be stressed enough that you should always take some sort of backup in case of equipment failure. It is very frustrating to have put in so much effort and then have to abort the chosen delivery method. But it happens to the best of us. So be prepared to resort to a more traditional method, such as overhead projectors.

1.2 Transferring the presentation

If you are using a computer other than that on which you prepared the presentation, you will need to copy it onto another medium to transfer it – for example, floppy disk, Zip disk, CD-ROM or transferred across a network. If you do not have a removable form of storage with a large enough capacity you will need to use the **Pack and Go Wizard**. This also enables you to use the file on a computer that does not have PowerPoint installed – although the computer will need to have Windows 95 or a more recent version of Windows.

1.3 Using Pack and Go

The **Pack and Go Wizard** guides you through copying a presentation file. **Pack and Go** compresses the file and enables you to save it to more than one floppy disk. (You will need to have a few ready. It is a good idea to number them so that they will be in the correct order when decompressing.) It creates two main files **Pres0.ppz** (the compressed presentation file) and **Pngsetup.exe** (this decompresses the file).

Handy reference

Pack and Go
File menu, **Pack and Go**.

METHOD

1   From the **File** menu, select: **Pack and Go**.
2   The **Pack and Go Wizard 1** is displayed (see Figure 9.1).
3   Click on: **Next**.
4   The **Pack and Go Wizard 2** is displayed (see Figure 9.2).

Figure 9.1 *Pack and Go Wizard 1*

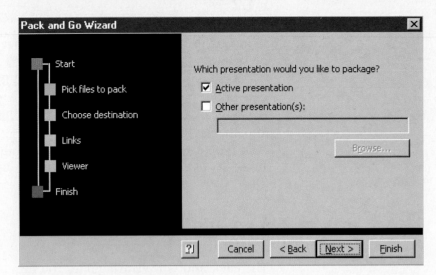

Figure 9.2 *Pack and Go Wizard 2*

5 Select the presentation you want to package.
6 Click on: **Next**.
7 The **Pack and Go Wizard 3** is displayed (see Figure 9.3).

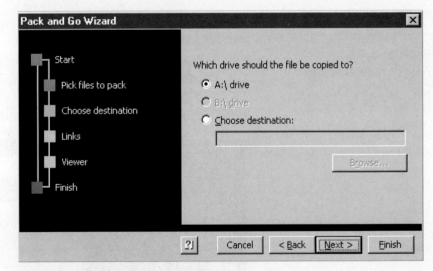

Figure 9.3 *Pack and Go Wizard 3*

8 Select where you want the file copied to.
9 Click on: **Next**.
10 The **Pack and Go Wizard 4** is displayed (see Figure 9.4).

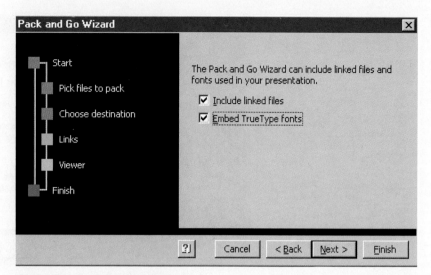

Figure 9.4 *Pack and Go Wizard 4*

11 Click in the box to **Include linked files**. (This will then include any sound, video and so on.)
12 Click in the box to **Embed TrueType fonts**. (This ensures that any fonts are reproduced correctly.)
13 Click on: **Next**.
14 The **Pack and Go Wizard 5** is displayed (see Figure 9.5).

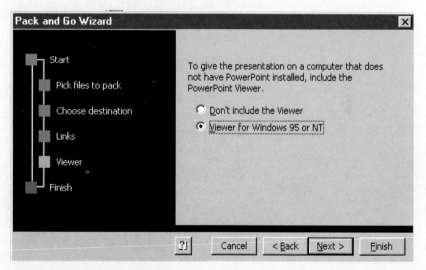

Figure 9.5 *Pack and Go Wizard 5*

15 Click in the option button **Viewer for Windows 95 or NT** if you know that PowerPoint is not installed on the computer that you will be using to show the presentation.
16 Click on: **Next**.
17 The **Pack and Go Wizard 6** is displayed (see Figure 9.6).

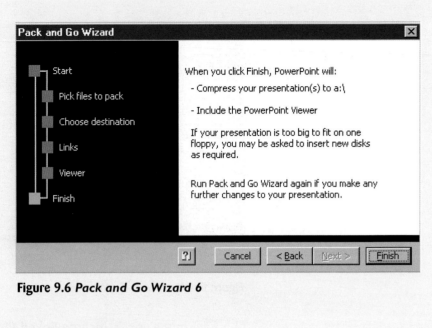

Pack and Go Wizard

Start
Pick files to pack
Choose destination
Links
Viewer
Finish

When you click Finish, PowerPoint will:
- Compress your presentation(s) to a:\
- Include the PowerPoint Viewer

If your presentation is too big to fit on one floppy, you may be asked to insert new disks as required.

Run Pack and Go Wizard again if you make any further changes to your presentation.

?| Cancel   < Back   Next >   Finish

Figure 9.6 Pack and Go Wizard 6

18   Click on: **Finish**.
19   Insert floppy disks when prompted.

1.4 Running the presentation

METHOD

1   Click on the **Pngsetup.exe** file on the floppy disk. (When this file is run it will decompress the presentation.)
2   Select the destination location.
3   Click on: **OK**.
4   Select: to view the presentation.

If you examine the folder where the decompressed files are stored, you will see that a number of files have been created during the **Pack and Go** process. Double-click on the file **Ppview.exe** to start the PowerPoint viewer. Double-click the name of the presentation. At the end of the slide show, click on the **End Show** button.

(See the **Appendix** for other ways to present a show and suggestions to try if your presentation is not running as you want.)

2 Preparing yourself for delivering the presentation

Learning objectives

- Rehearsal
- Cope with nerves
- Prepare your voice
- Deliver the presentation
- Deal with interruptions
- Take questions
- Final note

2.1 Rehearsal

Rehearsing the presentation in the actual room with the actual equipment that you will be using is extremely helpful. Not only does this help overcome any nerves, but also ensures you have everything adjusted correctly. If you do not have access to the room and equipment then it is still worth rehearsing. Try to arrange for a couple of colleagues or family members to make up the audience. Their input can be constructive and reassuring. Do not be surprised if they have criticisms of the way you do things. (Negative comments can also be constructive.) You can ponder whether their criticism is valid and, if so, think of ways to improve. Any positive comments are, of course, a welcome morale booster.

Rehearsing gives a chance to check the timing of each section. Remember that most presentations are usually longer than you have rehearsed. You will have a chance to discover if there are any points that you are unsure of, and you can remedy these. You can also decide on appropriate body language and how to change the tone of your voice to make things more interesting.

2.2 Coping with nerves

It is normal to feel nervous, even verging on the edge of panic. Feeling nervous can be a good thing and will key you up for a good performance. Try some relaxation techniques like closing your eyes and deep breathing. Knowing that you have prepared well for this moment and have checked and double-checked the equipment will make things less stressful. Act calm and stay in control and nobody will notice your nerves. Once you get started on 'your topic' you will most probably forget yourself, concentrate on your topic and you might even enjoy the presentation.

2.3 Preparing your voice

If you are nervous your throat can become dry. Sucking a sweet beforehand and ensuring you have some water handy when delivering the presentation (not iced as this can tighten the throat) will help. It is a good idea to prepare your voice by talking to someone or, if there is nobody about, speaking aloud the words of a song or poem. When delivering the presentation, project your voice by keeping your head up, exaggerating your speech – for example, mouth open wider than in normal conversation, using clear consonants and speaking slowly. If you mumble and rush, the audience will have a difficult job straining to understand. Alter the tone and volume to emphasise important points. Most speakers feel worried that they may dry up. Remember that occasional silences at the correct time can help the audience ponder what has been said so far.

2.4 Delivering the presentation

Try to arrive at the venue early so that you have time to cope with anything unexpected and avoid having to start off with an apology (this is always detrimental). If your presentation is topical ensure you have heard the latest news and consider how you might add this news to your presentation (if you think it merits it). It is good to get off to the best start. Try to look relaxed and confident and smile. Do not rush to get started. Aim to be natural and be yourself.

It is courteous to thank the chairperson who has probably introduced you. If not you will need to introduce yourself. This should be done very briefly. State whether there will be a break, when you will be taking questions and when the presentation will finish. Avoid the urge to look down at your notes. Maintaining eye contact with the audience especially at the beginning is essential. Try to be as personal, friendly, courteous and unpompous as possible.

2.5 Dealing with interruptions

If anything happens to interrupt your presentation, when restarting, recap on the main points so that everyone knows where you are starting from (including you).

2.6 Taking questions

In a formal situation, you will have made explicit when the question session will be. Try to stick to it. If you have interruptions, repeat that you will address any questions at the end. Do not act annoyed or belittle the questioner. Try to interpret why the question has been asked so that you can best answer it. You may need to repeat a question for the benefit of people at the back who may not have heard it and this will also give you a bit more time to think about the answer. If you are unable to answer a question, say so and promise to get back later. It is better than some garbled reply. Alternatively, gesture to a colleague who may be able to respond. Keep the answers quite short (but not too short) so that there is ample time for other questions.

2.7 And finally

Always try to end on a strong and optimistic note if the topic merits it. Give out any handouts and remember to thank everyone concerned.

PowerPoint 2000 Quick Reference

Action	Keyboard	Mouse	Right-mouse menu	Menu
Action buttons, add				**Slide Show, Action Buttons**
Action Settings			**Action Settings**	**Slide Show, Action Settings**
Alignment, in relation to slide		Select object **Drawing** toolbar, **Draw**, **Align or Distribute**, **Relative to Slide** then **Draw**, **Align** or **Distribute**, select option you want	**Format Placeholder**, **Position** tab (enables exact positioning)	**Format, Placeholder**, **Position** tab
AutoContent Wizard		Select from opening dialog box		**File, New**, General tab, **AutoContent Wizard**
AutoLayout, change		Formatting toolbar, Click: the **Common Tasks** button, then **Slide Layout**	**Slide Layout**	**Format, Slide Layout**
Background, customise			**Background**	**Format, Background**
Bold text	**Ctrl + B**	Click: the **B** **Bold** button	**Font**	**Format, Font**
			Select: **Bold** from the **Font** style: menu	
Borders		Select object **Drawing** toolbar, Click: the 🖉 **Line Color** button Click: the ≡ **Line Style** button	**Format Placeholder**	**Format, Placeholder**
Bullets, change type			**Bullets and Numbering**	**Format, Bullets and Numbering**

Action	Keyboard	Mouse	Right-mouse menu	Menu
Capitals (blocked), when keying in	**Caps Lock**, key in the text, **Caps Lock** again to key in lower case text			
keyed in text	Select text to be changed			
				For**mat**, Change Cas**e**, **UPPERCASE**
Centre text	Select the text			
	Ctrl + E	Click: the ☰ **Center** button		Fo**rmat**, **Alignment**, **C**enter
Change case	Select the text to be changed From the **Format** menu, select: **Change Cas**e Select the appropriate case			
Chart, insert using AutoLayout	Select appropriate slide **AutoLayout**, i.e. chart or organisation chart Data chart – overwrite sample data, click: ▦ **View Datasheet** button Organisation – key in text. **File** menu, **Exit and Return to (presentation)**			
insert	Data chart – **Insert**, **C**hart *or* click: 📊 **Insert Chart** button Organisation – **Insert**, **O**bject, Create **n**ew, MS Organization Chart 2.0			
Clip art insert,		Click: the 🖼 **Insert Clip Art** button		**Insert**, **P**icture, **Cl**ip Art
group		**Drawing** toolbar, **Draw**, **Group**	**G**rouping, **G**roup	
ungroup		**Drawing** toolbar, **Draw**, **Ungroup**	**G**rouping, **U**ngroup	
Close a file	**Ctrl + W**	Click: the ✕ **Close** button		**F**ile, **C**lose
Colours, slide			Slide **C**olor Scheme	Fo**rmat**, Slide **C**olor Scheme

Action	Keyboard	Mouse	Right-mouse menu	Menu
Custom animation	In **Slide** or **Normal View**			
			Cus<u>t</u>om Animation	**Sli<u>d</u>e Show, Cust<u>o</u>m Animation**
Cut text	Select the text to be cut			
	Ctrl + X	Click: the ✂ **Cut** button	**Cu<u>t</u>**	**<u>E</u>dit, Cut**
Delete a character	Press: **Delete** to delete the character to the right of the cursor Press: ◄— (backspace) to delete the character to the left of the cursor			
Delete an image	Select the image, press: **Delete**			
Delete a word	Double-click: on the word to select it. Press: **Delete**			
Delete a slide	Select the slide in **Slide Sorter View**. Press: **Delete**			
Delete/cut a block of text	Select the text you want to delete			
	Delete *or* **Ctrl ᵢ X**	Click: the ✂ **Cut** button	**Cu<u>t</u>**	**<u>E</u>dit, Cut**
Design Templates		Formatting toolbar, **<u>C</u>ommon Tasks, Appl<u>y</u> Design Template**		**F<u>o</u>rmat, Apply Design Template**
Display, guides ruler				**<u>V</u>iew, <u>G</u>uides**
				<u>V</u>iew, <u>R</u>uler
Duplicate slide	**<u>I</u>nsert** menu, **<u>D</u>uplicate Slide**			
Effects, transitional timings	In **Slide Sorter** view			
		Click: the ⬚ **Slides Transition** button	**Slide <u>T</u>ransition**	**Sli<u>d</u>e Show, Slide <u>T</u>ransition**
	In the **Advance** section Select: the timing you require			

Action	Keyboard	Mouse	Right-mouse menu	Menu
Effects, transitional effects	In **Slide Sorter** view			
		Click: the ▼ down arrow next to **Slide Transition Effects** box	**Slide Transition**	**Slide Show, Slide Transition**
	In the **Advance** section Select: the timing you require			
Effects, preset animation	In **Slide Sorter** view			
		Click: the ▼ down arrow next to **Text Preset Animation**	**Slide Transition**	**Slide Show, Slide Transition**
			In the **Effects** section	
	Select: the effect you want from the drop-down menu			
Exit PowerPoint	Alt + F4	Click: the ✕ Close button		**File, Exit**
Font	Select the text you want to change			
		Click: the ▼ down arrow next to **Font** box Select: the font you require	**Font**	**Format, Font**
			Select: the required font from the **Font:** menu	
Font size	Select the text you want to change			
		Click: the ▼ down arrow next to **Font Size** box Select: the font you require	**Font**	**Format, Font**
			Select: the required size from the **Size:** menu	
Serif	Serif fonts have small lines at upper and lower ends of characters – e.g. **Times New Roman**			
Sans serif	Sans serif fonts do not have lines – e.g. **Arial**			

Action	Keyboard	Mouse	Right-mouse menu	Menu
Formatting, copy		Click: the **Format Painter** button		
Headers and footers				**View**, **Header and Footer**
Help	F1			**Help** **Microsoft PowerPoint Help**
	Shift + F1			What's **This?**
Hide a slide		In **Slide Sorter View**, click: the **Hide Slide** button	In **Slide Sorter View**, **Hide Slide**	**Slide Show**, **Hide Slide**
Hyperlinks, add button	Ctrl + K	Click: the **Insert Hyperlink**	**Hyperlink**	**Insert**, **Hyperlink**
Import graphic media clip				**Insert**, **Picture** or **Object**
				Insert, **Movies and Sounds**
extract text, Excel graph or other object	Use **copy** (in the source application) and **paste** into PowerPoint			
from scanner or camera				**Insert**, **Picture from Scanner or Camera**
Insert text	Position the cursor where you want the text to appear. Key in the text			
Insert, slide from file				**Insert**, **Slides From Files**
Line Spacing				**Format**, **Line Spacing**
Lines, add format	Use the relevant **Drawing** toolbar buttons			

Action	Keyboard	Mouse	Right-mouse menu	Menu
Load PowerPoint	In Windows desktop			
		Double-click: the **PowerPoint** shortcut icon		**Start**, **Programs**, **Microsoft PowerPoint**
Master Slide(s) Slide Master Title Master				**View**, **Master**, **Slide Master**
				View, **Master**, **Title Master**
Narration, record				**Slide Show**, **Record Narration**
New presentation, create	**Ctrl + N**	Click: the ▢ **New** button		**File**, **New**
New Slide	**Ctrl + M**	Click: the 🗐 **New Slide** button		**Insert**, **New Slide**
Notes, add	In **Normal View/Outline View**, add to the **Notes** pane			
Number slides				**Insert**, **Slide Number**
Objects, insert				Select from **Insert**
Open an existing file	**Ctrl + O**	Click: the 📂 **Open** button		**File**, **Open**
	Select the appropriate directory and file name Click: **Open**			
Orientation of slides				**File**, **Page Setup**
Outline View (see Chapter 2, Section 2) demote promote	**Ctrl + Enter**	Click: the ➡ **Demote** button		
		Click: the ⬅ **Promote** button		
new slide	**Enter**			

Action	Keyboard	Mouse	Right-mouse menu	Menu
remove bullets	**Shift + Enter**			
Pack and Go				**and Go**
Page setup				**File, Page Setup**
Placeholder, delete				**Edit, Cut**
Print – Slides, Handouts, Notes Pages, Outline View	**Ctrl + P**			**File, Print**
	Select from the **Print what:** drop-down menu			
Projector Wizard				**Slide Show, Set Up Show**
Redo		Click: the ↶ ▾ **Redo** button		**Edit**, make selection
Remove text emphasis	Select text to be changed			
	Ctrl + B (remove bold) **Ctrl + I** (remove italics) **Ctrl + U** (remove underline)	Click: the appropriate button: **B** **I** **U**	**Font**	**Format, Font**
			Select **Regular** from the **Font Style:** menu	
Resize objects	Select the object. Resize using the handles. To preserve aspect ratio, resize from a corner.			
Run slide show		Click: the 🖥 **Slide Show** button at bottom left of screen		**View, Slide Show**
Save	**Ctrl + S**	Click: the 💾 **Save** button		**File, Save**
	If you have not already saved the file you will be prompted to specify the directory and to name the file.			

Action	Keyboard	Mouse	Right-mouse menu	Menu
Save using a different name or to a different directory or in a different format				**File**, **Save As**
	Select the appropriate drive and change the file name and file type if relevant. Click: **Save**			
Select All	**Ctrl + A**			**Edit**, **Select All**
Shadow, add	On the **Drawing** toolbar, click: the 🔲 **Shadow** button			
Slide order	In **Slide Sorter View** Click and drag the slide to required position or use cut and paste			
Slide Master				**View**, **Master**, **Slide Master**
Slides, write on				**Slide Show**, **Set Up Show**
Special characters, insert				**Insert**, **Symbol**
Spell check	**F7**	Click: the 🔤 **Spelling** button		**Tools**, **Spelling**
Superscript and subscript text			**Font, Effects**	**Format, Font, Effects**
Table, insert		Click and drag down: the 🔲 **Insert Table** button		**Insert, Table**
Title Master				**View**, **Master**, **Title Master**
Toolbars, modify	**View**, **Toolbars**, **Customize**			
Undo	**Ctrl + Z**	Click: the ↶ ▾ **Undo** button		Edit, make selection
View		Click: a **View** button: 🔲🔲🔲🔲🔲		**View**, make selection

Action	Keyboard	Mouse	Right-mouse menu	Menu
WordArt		Click: **4** **Insert WordArt** button on the **Drawing** toolbar		**I**nsert, **P**icture, **W**ordArt
Zoom		Click: `57%` ▼ **Zoom** button		**V**iew, **Z**oom

Keyboard shortcuts

Keyboard	Menu
F1	Help
F7	Tools, Spelling
Ctrl + N	File, New
Ctrl + O	File, Open
Ctrl + S	File, Save
F12	File, Save As
Ctrl + W	File, Close
Ctrl + P	File, Print
Alt + F4	File, Exit
Ctrl + X	Edit, Cut
Ctrl + C	Edit, Copy
Ctrl + V	Edit, Paste
Ctrl + Z	Edit, Undo
Ctrl + A	Edit, Select All
Esc	Cancels items

Don't forget: Right-clicking over objects displays pop-up menus.

Glossary

This glossary gives a short description of commonly used computing and PowerPoint terms used throughout the book.

alignment positioning of text or graphics on a page in relation to other elements

application another word for 'program' or 'application program' – an application enables you to do something specific, e.g. word processing, payroll.

aspect ratio the ratio of width to height of an object – maintaining the aspect ratio means not making the object taller or wider

AutoLayout slide layouts with predefined placeholders

browser program that enables you to view web pages on the Internet

bullets small graphic, e.g. ● or ■, used to emphasise and separate items in a list

buttons using the mouse, you click on buttons to select actions – there are toolbar buttons, dialogue box buttons and so on.

CD-ROM removable storage medium that can hold large amounts of data, e.g. an entire encyclopaedia

character formatting changing a character's look by altering font, size, style and so on

chart graphical display of information, e.g. bar chart, organisational chart

clicking pressing and releasing the left mouse button

clip art artwork that is available for you to insert into documents

clipboard where the computer stores items you have copied or cut, ready to paste somewhere else

cursor symbol (which changes shape depending on what you are doing) displayed on the screen, showing where the next character will be displayed

design template professionally designed template including colour scheme, layout, font formatting and so on

dialogue box window that is displayed asking you for information

document file containing text or pictures

double-clicking quickly pressing and releasing the left mouse button twice

dragging moving things around using the mouse

drive device that reads and writes onto disks

file unit of information stored on the computer, e.g. a PowerPoint file, a Word file, an Excel file

file name + extensions name given to a file – the extension is the letters after the file name that allow the computer to identify its type: PowerPoint files have **ppt** extensions

floppy disk portable storage medium that is floppy, but protected by having a plastic case

folder storage location to keep related files together – sometimes known as a 'directory'

font character set with predefined styles and sizes – e.g. Times New Roman, Arial

handouts printed pages containing slides – can be several per page

header and footer special areas at the top and bottom of pages for information that can appear on all slides in a presentation or on pages in printouts – e.g. handouts

Help press **F1** to access information on topics you are unsure of

hover place the mouse pointer over an object for a few seconds

icon small pictures that represent objects in a graphical user interface (GUI)

margin distance of text and graphics from the edges of printed pages

master slides slides on which all slides in the presentation are based – allows global formatting; each presentation has a slide master, title master, handout master and notes master

menu list of commands grouped into related tasks from which you can choose
drop-down (*or pull-down*) displayed from top of screen downward when selected
pop-up usually activated using the right mouse button – pops up on screen

menu bar row of menu options

object content on slides and in placeholders – e.g. clip art, chart

OHP overhead projector

outline text of the slide

panes when a window is split into several parts, each part is called a pane

placeholder boxes in which to insert content of slides

pointer symbol on the screen that moves when you move the mouse or another pointing device

presenter notes printed pages containing slides and notes

print queue when more than one document has been sent to the printer, a print queue forms so documents are stored and printed in turn – print queues are common on networks

recycle bin deleted files are sent to the recycle bin – they can be recovered from here if necessary, depending on the set up; files deleted from floppy disks are not sent to the recycle bin

right-click click the right mouse button – usually reveals context-sensitive menu

scrollbar horizontal or vertical strip that appears on right or bottom of window and lets you move through a document using the mouse to reveal previously hidden parts that couldn't fit in the window

slide name for pages created in PowerPoint

slide show displaying slides one after the other

select highlight a portion of text or an object on screen so you can manipulate it

spellcheck command that compares spelling in a document with that in the program's dictionary

subfolder folder within a folder

tab (in text) pre-set position for aligning text

taskbar strip (usually) along bottom of windows desktop containing **Start** button, icons for all active tasks, quick launch icons and system tray

template a blank document with pre-set styles and page layout settings which you can use to create a document

text box box you can create on a slide in which to insert text

toolbar line of buttons containing clickable short-cut icons

undo command that reverses your most recent action(s)

Web see World Wide Web

window rectangular screen area in which applications and documents are displayed

wizard facility to help achieve a task by leading you through steps involved

word wrap word-processing feature that automatically starts a new line when text reaches end of current line

World Wide Web visible part of the Internet containing linked html documents accessed through browsers – often abbreviated to 'the Web'

Zip disk removable storage medium that can hold a large amount of data – more than a floppy disk but less than a CD-ROM

Appendix

Copying a file from the CD-ROM

1 Insert the CD-ROM into the drive.
2 From the **Start** menu, select: **Run**.
3 The **Run** dialogue box is displayed.
4 In the **Open** box, key in: the CD-ROM drive – e.g. **D:**
5 Click on: **OK**.
6 The contents of the CD-ROM are displayed.
7 Locate the relevant file. (If the file is contained in a folder, you will need to open the folder by double-clicking on it to display the file name.)
8 Right-click on the file.
9 Select: **Copy** from the pop-up menu.
10 Click on the down arrow of the **Address** box and click on the destination location.
11 Right-click in a white space in the destination location window.
12 Select: **Paste** from the pop-up menu.

Note: You can copy more than one file at a time by holding down the **Ctrl** key when selecting files.

Office Assistant

Hiding the Office Assistant

1 Right-click on the Office Assistant.
2 Select: **Options** and set them to your preferences.
3 Click on: **OK**.

Turning the Office Assistant on

From the **Help** menu, select: **Show the Office Assistant**.

Checking spelling and style

There are many options available. Throughout the book, I have chosen not to check on an ongoing basis but after keying in entire documents. Should you wish to choose other options:

1 From the **Tools** menu, select: **Options**.
2 Click on: the **Spelling & Style** tab.

3 Select your preferences.
4 Click on: **OK**.

Note: Many other PowerPoint options can be set by selecting **Options** on the **Tools** menu.

More ways of presenting PowerPoint shows

Online meeting	**Tools** menu, **Online Collaboration**
Broadcasting over the web	**Slide Show** menu, **Online Broadcast**
Publishing on the web	**File** menu, **Save as Web Page**
E-mail a presentation	**File** menu, **Send To**

Saving in different file formats

Presentation	The Default – a typical PowerPoint presentation
PowerPoint 95, 97-2000, 4.0	Other versions of PowerPoint
Web page	For displaying on the Internet, will open in a web browser
Design template	Saves as a template
PowerPoint Show	PowerPoint opens this file in **Slide Show View** and runs and closes the show
GIF Graphics Interchange Format	Saves the slide as a GIF file – GIF files are common on the web
JPEG File Interchange Format	Saves the slide as a JPG file – use this for any photographic material since it produces a good image
PNG Portable Network Graphics Format	PNG is another graphics format used on the web; it compresses and downloads well

Device Independent Bitmap	Changes the slide into BMP format that is pixel-based; it can then be imported into other applications
Windows Metafile	Changes the slide into WMF graphic format (a vector format) – this can be imported into other applications and resizes well
Outline/RTF	Saves only the text of the presentation so that it can be imported into another application – e.g. Word
Tag Image File Format	Changes the slide into TIFF – a bitmap graphics format that is widely recognised by other applications

PowerPoint file sizes

PowerPoint file sizes can become very big especially when adding graphics, sound and video.

Checking file size

From the **File** menu, select: **Properties**, **General** tab. When you run a presentation, PowerPoint does not load a page at a time but loads the whole file into memory. In addition, it creates a temporary file in the process, before saving this temporary file over the existing file. The size of file that the computer can deal with adequately will be determined by the amount of RAM and virtual memory that the computer has. To be on the safe side, do not let file sizes become more than 100 MB at most and seriously consider if you could reduce the size any more. If not, then it is probably best to convert the presentation into two presentations that you run consecutively.

Fonts

When you transfer your presentation to another computer, the destination computer may not have all of the fonts installed. The standard fonts Arial and Times New Roman are not a problem, but more unusual fonts can be. To overcome this problem you can embed fonts:

1   With the presentation file open on the original computer, from the **File** menu, select: **Save As**.
2   In the **Save As** dialogue box, click on the **Tools** button.

3   Select: **Embed TrueType Fonts**.
4   Save the file in the normal way.

Sound

Your computer's speakers may not be loud enough to reach the whole audience. You may need to use external speakers for your computer or an external sound system.

Projection problems?

- Is the cable between the projector and the video output connector on your computer properly connected?
- If you are using a laptop computer have you pressed the appropriate function key to activate the video output?
- Did you connect and turn on the projector before you turned on the computer? If not your computer may not have recognised that the projector is connected.
- Have you adjusted your computer's display settings to match the projector resolutions via **Windows Control Panel**? (See **Chapter 8, Section 1**.)
- Does your projector go blank during pauses in the presentation? Turn off all screen savers and other power saving utilities in **Windows Power Management** utility.

Contents of CD-ROM

Milton Keynes presentation
This folder contains a multimedia presentation about Milton Keynes. Double-click on **Milton Keynes.ppt** *to open the PowerPoint file, then from the* **View** *menu, select* **Slide Show** *to view the presentation. Press:* **Esc** *when you have finished.*

Photos and ClipArt
This folder contains many photos and ClipArt images that you can use in your presentations.

Academic Reading Rooms.ppt	Hotel.ppt
Accountants.ppt	Insurance.ppt
Art debate.ppt	Motor.ppt
Carlton Green.doc	Numerical data.ppt
Colour.ppt	Picture toolbar.ppt
Cosy cafe.ppt	Playgroup.ppt
Dust mites.doc	Sleep.ppt
Effects.ppt	Slide Shows.ppt
Good and bad practice.ppt	Swimming.ppt
	Village show.ppt

Whirlwind tour – creating a basic PowerPoint presentation

Loading PowerPoint

Start menu, **Programs**, **Microsoft PowerPoint** or double-click on the
PowerPoint shortcut icon if you have one.

Creating slide 1

1 Click on **Blank Presentation** then on: **OK**.
2 Select: **Title Slide AutoLayout**.
3 Click on: **OK**.
4 Change to **Slide View** by clicking on the ⬚ **Slide View** button.
5 Click in the top placeholder (**Click to add title**) and key in the title of your presentation.
6 Click in the bottom placeholder (**Click to add subtitle**) and key in your name or a subtitle.

Formatting the text on slide 1

Select the text you want to format and then use the **Formatting** toolbar buttons and/or the **Format** menu, selecting: **Font**.

Saving the presentation

1 **File** menu, select: **Save As**.
2 Select where you want to save the file and key in a file name.
3 Click on: **Save**.

Adding a bulleted list to a specified slide layout

1 Click on: the ⬚ **New Slide** button.
2 Select: **Text and ClipArt AutoLayout**.
3 Click on: **OK**.
4 In the **Click to add title** placeholder, key in the slide title.
5 In the left-hand placeholder, key in your bulleted items, pressing **Enter** after each (except the last one). Notice that a bulleted list has been created.

Inserting a graphical image to a specified slide AutoLayout

1   In the right-hand placeholder, double-click in the placeholder.
2   Scroll through the **ClipArt** and decide which one to use.
3   Right-click on the chosen one and then click on: the 🖼 **Insert ClipArt** button.
4   Resize the graphical image by dragging the handles.

Adding text to a blank AutoLayout

1   Click on the 🗐 **New Slide** button.
2   Select: **Blank AutoLayout**.
3   Click on: **OK**.
4   Click on the 📰 **Text Box** button on the **Drawing** toolbar.
5   Click where you want the text to start.
6   Key in the text and format it as required.
7   Click in any white space on the slide when finished.
8   Adjust the text box size so that the text fits neatly on the slide.

Adding graphics to a blank AutoLayout

1   **Insert** menu, select: **Picture** and then **ClipArt**.
2   Right-click on the clip art you want to insert.
3   Click on: the **Insert clip** button.
4   Resize the graphic using the handles.
5   Reposition using the *drag and drop* method.

Index